Alfred J. Church

Stories From Homer

Alfred J. Church

Stories From Homer

ISBN/EAN: 9783337015466

Printed in Europe, USA, Canada, Australia, Japan

Cover: Foto ©Thomas Meinert / pixelio.de

More available books at **www.hansebooks.com**

MORNING

STORIES FROM HOMER

BY THE

REV. ALFRED J. CHURCH, M.A.,

Head Master of King Edward's School, Retford;

AUTHOR OF "STORIES FROM VIRGIL."

WITH TWENTY-FOUR ILLUSTRATIONS

FROM FLAXMAN'S DESIGNS.

EIGHTH THOUSAND

SEELEY, JACKSON & HALLIDAY, FLEET STREET,
LONDON. MDCCCLXXVIII.

UNWIN BROTHERS, PRINTERS, CHILWORTH AND LONDON.

To my Wife,

WITHOUT WHOSE ENCOURAGEMENT
IT WOULD NOT HAVE BEEN WRITTEN,
THIS BOOK IS DEDICATED.

PREFACE.

These "Stories" will, I hope, represent Homer not unfaithfully to readers, old and young, who do not know him in the original; may, perhaps, commend him to some of the younger sort who, having made acquaintance with him, do not find this acquaintance tend to love.

We have given by way of illustration some of Flaxman's famous designs. These we have ventured to colour, hoping that by so doing we should render them more attractive, without transgressing any rule of art. The style of the outlines was suggested by the Etruscan vase painting, and Flaxman himself did some work of a similar kind for Wedgwood. Most of the vase paintings are in black and red, but there is authority for the employment of the buff tint.

CONTENTS.

THE ILIAD.

CHAP.		PAGE
I.	THE QUARREL OF THE CHIEFS	1
II.	THE BROKEN COVENANT	17
III.	THE BATTLE IN THE PLAIN	27
IV.	HECTOR AND ANDROMACHÉ	46
V.	THE DUEL OF HECTOR AND AJAX	54
VI.	THE ADVENTURE OF ULYSSES AND DIOMED	64
VII.	THE WOUNDING OF THE CHIEFS	76
VIII.	THE BATTLE AT THE WALL	83
IX.	THE BATTLE AT THE SHIPS	92
X.	THE BATTLE AT THE SHIPS (*continued*)	100
XI.	THE DEEDS AND DEATH OF PATROCLUS	109
XII.	THE ROUSING OF ACHILLES	119
XIII.	THE BATTLE AT THE RIVER	129
XIV.	THE DEATH OF HECTOR	141
XV.	THE RANSOMING OF HECTOR	156

THE ODYSSEY.

CHAP.		PAGE
I.	THE CYCLOPS	177
II.	THE ISLAND OF ÆOLUS—THE LÆSTRYGONS—CIRCÉ	193
III.	THE REGIONS OF THE DEAD—SCYLLA—THE OXEN OF THE SUN—CALYPSO	205
IV.	TELEMACHUS AND PENELOPÉ	214
V.	NESTOR AND MENELAÜS	222
VI.	ULYSSES ON HIS RAFT	236
VII.	NAUSICAA AND ALCINOÜS	245
VIII.	ULYSSES AND THE SWINEHERD	261
IX.	THE RETURN OF TELEMACHUS	271
X.	ULYSSES IN HIS HOME	279
XI.	THE TRIAL OF THE BOW	292
XII.	THE SLAYING OF THE SUITORS	300

LIST OF ILLUSTRATIONS.

MORNING ... ... *Frontispiece*	
ATHENÉ SUPPRESSING THE FURY OF ACHILLES ...	8
DIOMED CASTING HIS SPEAR AGAINST ARES	42
THE MEETING OF HECTOR AND ANDROMACHÉ ...	50
HECTOR AND AJAX SEPARATED BY THE HERALDS ...	62
DIOMED AND ULYSSES RETURNING WITH THE SPOILS OF RHESUS	74
AJAX DEFENDING THE GREEK SHIPS AGAINST THE TROJANS	106
SLEEP AND DEATH CONVEYING THE BODY OF SARPEDON TO LYCIA	116
THETIS BRINGING THE ARMOUR TO ACHILLES ...	132
ANDROMACHÉ FAINTING ON THE WALL	154
ULYSSES GIVING WINE TO POLYPHEMUS	186
ULYSSES AT THE TABLE OF CIRCÉ	200

PENELOPÉ SURPRISED BY THE SUITORS	218
PENELOPÉ'S DREAM	234
ULYSSES FOLLOWING THE CAR OF NAUSICAA ...	250
ULYSSES WEEPS AT THE SONG OF DEMODOCUS ...	256
ULYSSES, ASLEEP, LAID ON HIS OWN COAST BY THE PHÆACIAN SAILORS	262
ULYSSES CONVERSING WITH EUMÆUS	266
ULYSSES AND HIS DOG	280
ULYSSES PREPARING TO FIGHT WITH IRUS ...	284
EURYCLEA DISCOVERS ULYSSES	290
PENELOPÉ CARRYING THE BOW OF ULYSSES TO THE SUITORS	294
ULYSSES KILLING THE SUITORS	302
THE MEETING OF ULYSSES AND PENELOPÉ	306

THE ILIAD

OR,

THE SIEGE OF TROY.

CHAPTER I.

THE QUARREL OF THE CHIEFS.

For nine years and more the Greeks had besieged the city of Troy, and being many in number and better ordered, and having very strong and valiant chiefs, they had pressed the men of the city very hard, so that these durst not go outside the walls. And, indeed, they might have taken it without further loss, but that there arose a deadly strife between two of the chiefs, even between Agamemnon, King of Mycenæ, who was sovereign lord of all the host; and Achilles, who was the bravest and most valiant man therein. Now the strife chanced in this wise.

The Greeks, having been away from home now many years, were in great want of things needful. Wherefore it was their custom to leave a part of their army to watch the city, and to send a part to spoil such towns in the country round about as they knew to be friendly to the men of Troy, or as they thought to contain good store of provision or treasure. "Are not all these," they were wont to say, "towns of the barbarians, and therefore lawful prey to men that are Greeks?" Now among the towns with which they dealt in this fashion was Chrysa, which was sacred to Apollo, who had a great temple therein and a priest. The temple and the priest the Greeks, fearing the anger of the god, had not harmed; but they had carried off with other prisoners the priest's daughter, Chryseïs by name. These and the rest of the spoil they divided among the kings, of whom there were many in the army, ruling each his own people. Now King Agamemnon, as being sovereign lord, went not commonly with the army at such times, but rather stayed behind, having charge of the siege that it should not be neglected. Yet did he always receive, as indeed was fitting, a share of the spoil. This time the Greeks gave him, with other things, the maiden Chryseïs. But there came to the camp next day the priest Chryses, wishing to ransom his daughter. Much gold he brought with him, and he had on his head the priest's crown, that men might reverence him the more. He went to all the chiefs, making his prayer that they would take the gold and give him back his daughter. And they all spake him fair, and would have done what he wished. Only Agamemnon would not have it so.

"Get thee out, greybeard!" he cried in great wrath. "Let me not find thee lingering now by the ships, neither coming hither again, or it shall be the worse for thee, for all thy priesthood. And as for thy daughter, I shall carry her away to Argos, when I shall have taken this city of Troy."

Then the old man went out hastily in great fear and trouble. And he walked in his sorrow by the shore of the sounding sea, and prayed to his god Apollo.

"Hear me, God of the silver bow. If I have built thee a temple, and offered thee the fat of many bullocks and rams, hear me, and avenge me on these Greeks!"

And Apollo heard him. Wroth he was that men had so dishonoured his priest, and he came down from the top of Olympus, where he dwelt. Dreadful was the rattle of his arrows as he went, and his presence was as the night coming over the sky. Then he shot the arrows of death, first on the dogs and the mules, and then on the men; and soon all along the shore rolled the black smoke from the piles of wood on which they burnt the bodies of the dead.

On the tenth day Achilles, who was the bravest and strongest of all the Greeks, called the people to an assembly. When they were gathered together he stood up among them and spake to Agamemnon.

"Surely it were better to return home, than that we should all perish here by the plague. But come, let us ask some prophet, or priest, or dreamer of dreams, why it is that Apollo is so wroth with us."

Then stood up Calchas, best of seers, who knew what had been, and what was, and what was to come, and spake.

"Achilles, thou biddest me tell the people why Apollo is wroth with them. Lo! I tell thee, but thou must first swear to stand by me, for I know that what I shall say will anger King Agamemnon, and it goes ill with common men when kings are angry."

"Speak out, thou wise man!" cried Achilles; "for I swear by Apollo that while I live no one shall lay hands on thee, no, not Agamemnon's self, though he be sovereign lord of the Greeks."

Then the prophet took heart and spake. "It is on behalf of his priest that Apollo is wroth, for he came to ransom his daughter, but Agamemnon would not let the maiden go. Now, then, ye must send her back to Chrysa without ransom, and with her a hundred beasts for sacrifice, so that the plague may be stayed."

Then Agamemnon stood up in a fury, his eyes blazing like fire.

"Never," he cried, "hast thou spoken good concerning me, ill prophet that thou art, and now thou tellest me to give up this maiden! I will do it, for I would not that the people should perish. Only take care, ye Greeks, that there be a share of the spoil for me, for it would ill beseem the lord of all the host that he alone should be without his share."

"Nay, my lord Agamemnon," cried Achilles, "thou art too eager for gain. We have no treasures out of which we may make up thy loss, for what we got out of the towns we have either sold or divided; nor would it be fitting that the people should give back what has been given to them. Give up the maiden, then, without conditions, and when we shall have taken this city of Troy, we will repay thee three and four fold."

"Nay, great Achilles," said Agamemnon, "thou shalt not cheat me thus. If the Greeks will give me such a share as I should have, well and good. But if not, I will take one for myself, whether it be from thee, or from Ajax, or from Ulysses; for my share I will have. But of this hereafter. Now let us see that this maiden be sent back. Let them get ready a ship, and put her therein, and with her a hundred victims, and let some chief go with the ship, and see that all things be rightly done."

Then cried Achilles, and his face was black as a thunder-storm, "Surely thou art altogether shameless and greedy, and, in truth, an ill ruler of men. No quarrel have I with the Trojans. They never harried oxen or sheep of mine. But I have been fighting in thy cause, and that of thy brother Menelaüs. Naught carest thou for that. Thou leavest me to fight, and sittest in thy tent at ease. But when the spoil is divided, thine is always the lion's share. Small indeed is my part—'a little thing, but dear.' And this, forsooth, thou wilt take away! Now am I resolved to go home. Small booty wilt thou get then, methinks!"

And King Agamemnon answered, "Go, and thy Myrmidons with thee! I have other chieftains as good as thou art, and ready, as thou art not, to pay me due respect. I hate thee, with thy savage, bloodthirsty ways. And as for the matter of the spoil, know that I will take thy share, the girl Briseïs, and fetch her myself, if need be, that all may know that I am sovereign lord here in the host of the Greeks."

Then Achilles was mad with anger, and he thought in his heart, "Shall I arise and slay this caitiff, or shall I keep down the wrath in my breast?" And as he thought he laid his hand on his sword-hilt, and had half drawn his sword from the scabbard, when lo! the goddess Athené stood behind him (for Heré, who loved both this chieftain and that, had sent her), and caught him by the long locks of his yellow hair. But Achilles marvelled much to feel the mighty grasp, and turned, and looked, and knew the goddess, but no one else in the assembly might see her. Then his eyes flashed with fire, and he cried, "Art thou come, child of Zeus, to see the insolence of Agamemnon? Of a truth, I think that he will perish for his folly."

But Athené said, "Nay, but I am come to stay thy wrath. Use bitter words, if thou wilt, but put up thy sword in its sheath, and strike him not. Of a truth, I tell thee that for this insolence of to-day he will bring thee hereafter splendid gifts, threefold and fourfold for all that he may take away."

Then Achilles answered, "I shall abide by thy command, for it is ever better for a man to obey the immortal gods." And as he spake he laid his heavy hand upon the hilt, and thrust back the sword into the scabbard, and Athené went her way to Olympus.

Then he turned him to King Agamemnon, and spake again. "Drunkard, with the eyes of a dog and the heart of a deer! never fighting in the front of the battle, nor daring to lie in the ambush! 'Tis a puny race thou rulest, or this had been thy last wrong. And as for

ATHENE REPRESSING THE FURY OF ACHILLES.

me, here is this sceptre: once it was the branch of a tree, but a cunning craftsman bound it with bronze to be the sign of the lordship which Zeus gives to kings; as surely as it shall never again have bark or leaves or shoot, so surely shall the Greeks one day miss Achilles, when they fall in heaps before the dreadful Hector, and thou shalt eat thy heart to think that thou hast wronged the bravest of thy host."

And as he spake he dashed his sceptre on the ground and sat down. And on the other side Agamemnon sat in furious anger. Then Nestor rose, an old man of a hundred years and more, and counselled peace. Let them listen, he said, to his counsel. Great chiefs in the old days, with whom no man now alive would dare to fight, had listened. Let not Agamemnon take away from the bravest of the Greeks the prize of war; let not Achilles, though he was mightier in battle than all other men, contend with Agamemnon, who was sovereign lord of all the hosts of Greece. But he spake in vain. For Agamemnon answered—

"Nestor, thou speakest well, and peace is good. But this fellow would lord it over all, and he must be taught that there is one here, at least, who is better than he."

And Achilles said, "I were a slave and a coward if I owned thee as my lord. Not so: play the master over others, but think not to master me. As for the prize which the Greeks gave me, let them do as they will. They gave it; let them take it away. But if thou darest to touch aught that is mine own, that hour thy life-blood shall redden on my spear."

Then the assembly was dismissed. Chryseïs was sent to her home with due offerings to the god, the wise Ulysses going with her. And all the people purified themselves, and the plague was stayed.

But King Agamemnon would not go back from his purpose. So he called to him the heralds, Talthybius and Eurybates, and said,

"Heralds, go to the tents of Achilles and fetch the maiden Briseïs. But if he will not let her go, say that I will come myself with many others to fetch her; so will it be the worse for him."

Sorely against their will the heralds went. Along the sea shore they walked, till they came to where, amidst the Myrmidons, were the tents of Achilles. There they found him sitting, but stood silent in awe and fear. But Achilles spied them, and cried aloud, "Come near, ye heralds, messengers of gods and men. 'Tis no fault of yours that ye are come on such an errand."

Then he turned to Patroclus (now Patroclus was his dearest friend) and said, "Bring the maiden from her tent, and let the heralds lead her away. But let them be witnesses, before gods and men, and before this evil-minded king, against the day when he shall have sore need of me to save his host from destruction. Fool that he is, who thinks not of the past nor of the future, that his people may be safe!"

Then Patroclus brought forth the maiden from her tent and gave her to the heralds. And they led her away, but it was sorely against her will that she went. But Achilles went apart from his comrades and sat upon the sea shore, falling into a great passion of tears, and stretching out his hands with loud prayer to his mother, who indeed was a goddess of the sea, Thetis by name. She heard him where she sat in the depths by her father, the old god of the sea, and rose—you would have thought it a mist rising—from the waves, and came to where he sat weeping, and stroked him with her hand, and called him by his name.

"What ails thee, my son?" she said.

Then he told her the story of his wrong, and when he had ended he said—

"Go, I pray thee, to the top of Olympus, to the palace of Zeus. Often have I heard thee boast how, long ago, thou didst help him when the other gods would have bound him, fetching Briareus of the hundred hands, who sat by him in his strength, so that the gods feared to touch him. Go now and call these things to his mind, and pray him that he help the sons of Troy and give them victory in the battle, so that the Greeks, as they flee before them, may have joy of this king of theirs, who has done such wrong to the bravest of his host."

And his mother answered him, "Surely thine is an evil lot, my son! Thy life is short, and it should of right be without tears and full of joy; but now it seems to me to be both short and sad. But I will go as thou sayest to Olympus, to the palace of Zeus, but not now, for he has gone, and the other gods with him, to a twelve days' feast with the pious Ethiopians. But when he comes back I will entreat and persuade him. And do thou sit still, nor go forth to battle."

When the twelve days were past, Thetis went to the top of Olympus, to the palace of Zeus, and made her prayer to him. He was loath to grant it, for he knew that it would anger his wife, Heré, who loved the Greeks and hated the sons of Troy. Yet he could not refuse her, but promised that it should be as she wished. And to make his word the surer, he nodded his awful head, and with the nod all Olympus was shaken.

That night Zeus took counsel with himself how he might best work his will. And he called to him a dream, and said, "Dream, go to the tent of Agamemnon, and tell him to set his army in array against Troy, for that the gods are now of one mind, and the day of doom is come for the city, so that he shall take it, and gain eternal glory for himself."

So the dream went to the tent of Agamemnon, and it took the shape of Nestor, the old chief, whom the king honoured more than all beside.

Then the false Nestor spake: "Sleepest thou, Agamemnon? It is not for kings to sleep all through the night, for they must take thought for many, and have many cares. Listen now to the words of Zeus: 'Set the battle in array against Troy, for the gods are now of one mind, and the day of doom is come for the city, and thou shalt take it, and gain eternal glory for thyself.'"

And Agamemnon believed the dream, and knew not the purpose of Zeus in bidding him go forth to battle, how that the Trojans should win the day, and great shame should come to himself, but great honour to Achilles, when all the Greeks should pray him to deliver them from death. So he rose from his bed and donned his tunic, and over it a great cloak, and fastened the sandals on his feet, and hung from his shoulders his mighty silver-studded sword, and took in his right hand the great sceptre of his house, which was the token of his sovereignty over all the Greeks. Then he went forth, and first took counsel with the chiefs, and afterwards called the people to the assembly. And after the assembly the shrill-voiced heralds called the host to the battle. As is the flare of a great fire when a wood is burning on a hill-top, so was the flash of their arms and their armour as they thronged to the field. And as the countless flocks of wild geese or cranes or swans now wheel and now settle in the great Asian fen by the stream of Cayster, or as the bees swarm in the spring, when the milk-pails are full, so thick the Greeks thronged to the battle in the great plain by the banks of the Scamander. Many nations were there, and many chiefs. But the most famous among them were these: Agamemnon, King of Mycenæ, and his brother, the yellow-haired Menelaüs, King of Sparta, and husband of the beautiful Helen; Ajax Oïleus, or, as men called him, the lesser Ajax, King of the Locri, swiftest of foot among the Greeks after the great Achilles; Ajax Telamon, from Salamis; Diomed, son of Tydeus, King of Argos, and with him Sthenelus; Nestor, King of Pylos, oldest and wisest among the Greeks; Ulysses, King of Ithaca, than whom there was no one more crafty in counsel; Idomeneus, grandson of the great judge Minos, King of Crete, and with him Meriones; Tlepolemus, son of Hercules, from Rhodes; Eumelus from Pheræ, son of that Alcestis who died for her husband and was brought back from death by Hercules. All these were there that day, and many more; and the bravest and strongest of all was Ajax, son of Telamon, and the best horses were the horses of Eumelus; but there was none that could compare with Achilles and the horses of Achilles, bravest man and swiftest steeds. Only Achilles sat apart, and would not go to the battle.

And on the other side the sons of Troy and their allies came forth from the gates of the city and set themselves in array. The most famous of their chiefs were these: Hector, son of King Priam, bravest and best of all; Æneas, son of Anchises and the goddess Aphrodité; Pandarus, from Mount Ida, with the bow which Apollo gave him; Asius, the son of Hyrtacus, who came from the broad salt river, the Hellespont; Pylæmenes, King of Paphlagonia; and Sarpedon from Lycia, whom men affirmed to be the son of Zeus himself, and with him Glaucus.

So the battle was set in array, and the two hosts stood over against each other.

CHAPTER II.

THE BROKEN COVENANT.

THEY were now about to fight, when from the ranks of the Trojans Paris rushed forth. He had a panther's skin over his shoulders, and a bow and a sword, and in either hand a spear, and he called aloud to the Greeks that they should send forth their bravest to fight with him. But when Menelaüs saw him he was glad, for he said that now he should avenge himself on the man who had done him such wrong. So a lion is glad when, being sorely hungered, he finds a stag or a wild goat; he devours it, and will not be driven from it by dogs or hunters. He leapt from his chariot and rushed to meet his enemy; but Paris, having done evil, and being therefore a coward in his heart, was afraid when he saw Menelaüs, and fled back into the ranks of his comrades, just as a man steps back in haste when unawares in a mountain glen he comes upon a snake. But Hector saw him and rebuked him. "Fair art thou to look upon, Paris, but nothing worth. Surely the Greeks will scorn us if they think that thou art our bravest warrior, because thou art of stately presence. But thou art a coward; and yet thou daredst to go across the sea and carry off the fair Helen. Why dost thou not stand and abide the onset of her husband, and see what manner of man he is? Little, I ween, would thy harp and thy long locks and thy fair face avail when thou wert lying in the dust! A craven race are the sons of Troy, or they would have stoned thee ere this."

Then Paris answered, "Thou speakest well, Hector, and thy rebuke is just. As for thee, thy heart is like iron, ever set on battle; yet are beauty and love also the gifts of the gods, and not to be despised. But now set Menelaüs and me in the midst, and let us fight, man to man, for the fair Helen and for all her possessions. And if he prevail over me, let him take her and them and depart, and the Greeks with him, but ye shall dwell in peace; but if I prevail they shall depart without her."

Then Hector was glad, and going before the Trojan ranks, holding his spear by the middle, he kept them back. But the Greeks would have thrown spears and stones at him, only Agamemnon cried aloud and said, "Hold: Hector has somewhat to say to us."

Then Hector said, "Hear, Trojans and Greeks, what Paris saith: Let all besides lay their arms upon the ground, and let Menelaüs and me fight for the fair Helen and all her wealth. And let him that is the better keep her and them, but the rest shall dwell in peace."

Then Menelaüs said, "The word pleaseth me well; let us fight together, and let us make agreement with oath and sacrifice. And because the sons of Priam are men of fraud and violence, let Priam himself come."

So they sent a herald to King Priam, but he sat on the wall with the old men. And as they talked, the fair Helen came near, and they said, "What wonder that men should suffer much for such a woman, for indeed she is divinely fair. Yet let her depart in the ships, nor bring a curse on us and our children."

But Priam called to her, "Come near, my daughter; tell me about these old friends of thine. For 'tis not thou, 'tis the gods who have brought about all this trouble. But tell me, who is this warrior that I see, so fair and strong? There are others even a head taller than he, but none of such majesty."

And Helen answered, "Ah, my father! would that I had died before I left husband and child to follow thy son. But as for this warrior, he is Agamemnon, a good king and brave soldier, and my brother-in-law in the old days."

"Happy Agamemnon," said Priam, "to rule over so many! Never saw I such an army gathered together, not even when I went to help the Phrygians when they were assembled on the banks of the Sangarus against the Amazons. But who is this that I see, not so tall as Agamemnon, but of broader shoulders? His arms lie upon the ground, and he is walking through the ranks of his men just as some great ram walks through a flock of sheep."

"This," said Helen, "is Ulysses of Ithaca, who is better in craft and counsel than all other men."

"'Tis well spoken, lady," said Antenor. "Well I remember Ulysses when he came hither on an embassy about thee with the brave Menelaüs. My guests they were, and I knew them well. And I remember how, in the assembly of the Trojans, when both were standing, Menelaüs was the taller, but when they sat, Ulysses was the more majestic to behold. And when they rose to speak, Menelaüs said few words, but said them wisely and well; and Ulysses—you had thought him a fool, so stiffly he held his sceptre and so downcast were his eyes; but as soon as he began, oh! the mighty voice, and the words thick as the falling snow!"

Then Priam said, " Who is that stalwart hero, so tall and strong, overtopping all by head and shoulders ? "

"That," said Helen, "is mighty Ajax, the bulwark of the Greeks. And next to him is Idomeneus. Often has Menelaüs had him as his guest in the old days, when he came from Crete. As for the other chiefs, I see and could name them all. But I miss my own dear brothers, Castor, tamer of horses, and Pollux, the mighty boxer. Either they came not from

Sparta, or, having come, shun the meeting of men for shame of me."

So she spake, and knew not that they were sleeping their last sleep far away in their dear fatherland. And when they had ended talking, the heralds came and told King Priam how that the armies called for him. So he went, and Antenor with him. And he on the one side, for the Trojans, and King Agamemnon for the Greeks, made a covenant with sacrifice that Paris and Menelaüs should fight together, and that the fair Helen, with all her treasures, should go with him who should prevail. And afterwards Hector and Ulysses marked out a space for the fight, and Hector shook two pebbles in a helmet, looking away as he shook them, that he whose pebble leapt forth the first should be the first to throw his spear. And it so befell that the lot of Paris leapt forth first. Then the two warriors armed themselves and came forth into the space, and stood over against each other, brandishing their spears, with hate in their eyes. Then Paris threw his spear. It struck the shield of Menelaüs, but pierced it not, for the spear point was bent back. Then

Menelaüs prayed to Zeus, "Grant, father Zeus, that I may avenge myself on Paris, who has done me this wrong: so shall men in after time fear to do wrong to their host." So speaking, he cast his long-shafted spear. It struck the shield of Paris and pierced it through, and passed through the corslet, and through the tunic, close to the loin; but Paris shrank aside, and the spear wounded him not. Then Menelaüs drew his silver-studded sword and struck a mighty blow on the top of the helmet of Paris, but the sword broke in four pieces in his hand. Then he cried in his wrath, "O Zeus, most mischief-loving of the gods, my spear I cast in vain, and now my sword is broken." Then he rushed forward and seized Paris by the helmet, and dragged him towards the host of the Greeks. And truly he had taken him, but Aphrodité loosed the strap that was beneath the chin, and the helmet came off in his hand. And Menelaüs whirled it among the Greeks and charged with another spear in his hand. But Aphrodité snatched Paris away, covering him with a mist, and put him down in his chamber in Troy. Then Menelaüs looked for him everywhere, but no one could tell him where he might be. No son of Troy would have hidden him out of kindness, for all hated him as death.

Then King Agamemnon said, "Now, ye sons of Troy, it is for you to give back the fair Helen and her wealth, and to pay me besides so much as may be fitting for all my cost and trouble."

But it was not the will of the gods that the sons of Troy should do this thing, but rather that their city should perish. So Athené took upon herself the shape of Laodocus, son of Antenor, and went to Pandarus, son of Lycaon, where he stood among his men. Then the false Laodocus said, "Pandarus, darest thou aim an arrow at Menelaüs? Truly the Trojans would love thee well, and Paris best of all, if they could see Menelaüs slain by an arrow from thy bow. Aim then, but first pray to Apollo, and vow that thou wilt offer a hundred beasts when thou returnest to thy city, Zeleia." Now Pandarus had a bow made of the horns of a wild goat which he had slain; sixteen palms long they were, and a cunning workman had made them smooth, and put a tip of gold whereon to fasten the bow-string. And Pandarus strung his bow, his comrades hiding him with their shields. Then he took an arrow from his quiver, and laid it on the bow-string, and drew the string to his breast, till the arrow-head touched the bow, and let fly. Right well aimed was the dart, but it was not the will of heaven that it should slay Menelaüs. It struck him, indeed, and passed through the belt and through the corslet and through the girdle, and pierced the skin. Then the red blood rushed out and stained the white skin, even as some Lycian or Carian woman stains the white ivory with red to adorn the war-horse of a king.

Sore dismayed was King Agamemnon to see the blood; sore dismayed also was the brave Menelaüs, till he spied the barb of the arrow, and knew that the wound was not deep. But Agamemnon cried—

"It was in an evil hour for thee, my brother, that I made a covenant with these false sons of Troy. Right well, indeed, I know that oath and sacrifice are not in vain, but will have vengeance at the last. Troy shall fall; but woe is me if thou shouldst die, Menelaüs. For the

Greeks will straight go back to their father-land, and the fair Helen will be left a boast to the sons of Troy, and I shall have great shame when one of them shall say, as he leaps on the tomb of the brave Menelaüs, 'Surely the great Agamemnon has avenged himself well; for he brought an army hither, but now is gone back to his home, but left Menelaüs here.' May the earth swallow me up before that day!"

"Nay," said Menelaüs, "fear not, for the arrow has but grazed the skin."

Then King Agamemnon bade fetch the physician. So the herald fetched Machaon, the physician. And Machaon came, and drew forth the arrow, and when he had wiped away the blood he put healing drugs upon the wound, which Chiron, the wise healer, had given to his father.

CHAPTER III.

THE BATTLE IN THE PLAIN.

But while this was doing, King Agamemnon went throughout the host, and if he saw any one stirring himself to get ready for the battle he praised him and gave him good encouragement; but whomsoever he saw halting and lingering and slothful, him he blamed and rebuked whether he were common man or chief. The last that he came to was Diomed, son of Tydeus with Sthenelus, son of Capaneus, standing by his side. And Agamemnon spake, "How is this, son of Tydeus ? Shrinkest thou from the battle ? This was not thy father's wont. I never saw him indeed, but I have heard that he was braver than all other men. Once he came to Mycenæ with great Polynices to gather allies against Thebes. And the men of Mycenæ would have sent them, only Zeus showed evil signs from heaven and forbade them. Then the Greeks sent Tydeus on an embassy to Thebes, where he found many of the sons of Cadmus feasting in the palace of Eteocles; but Tydeus was not afraid, though he was but one among many. He challenged them to contend with him in sport, and in everything he prevailed. But the sons of Cadmus bare it ill, and they laid an ambush for Tydeus as he went back, fifty men with two leaders—Mæon and Lycophon. But Tydeus slew them all, leaving only Mæon alive, that he might carry back the tidings to Thebes. Such was thy father; but his son is worse in battle, but better, it may be, in speech."

Nothing said Diomed, for he reverenced the king; but Sthenelus cried out, "Why speakest thou false, King Agamemnon, knowing the truth? We are not worse but better than our fathers. Did not we take Thebes, though we had fewer men than they, who indeed took it not?" But Diomed frowned and said, " Be silent, friend. I blame not King Agamemnon, that he rouses the Greeks to battle. Great glory will it be to him if they take the city, and great loss if they be worsted. But it is for us to be valiant."

So he passed through all the host. And the Greeks went forward to the battle, as the waves that curl themselves and then dash upon the shore, throwing high the foam. In order they went after their chiefs; you had thought them dumb, so silent were they. But the Trojans were like a flock of ewes which wait to be milked, and bleat hearing the voice of their lambs, so confused a cry went out from their army, for there were men of many tongues gathered together. And on either side the gods urged them on, but chiefly Athené the Greeks and Ares the sons of Troy. Then, as two streams in flood meet in some chasm, so the armies dashed together, shield on shield and spear on spear.

Antilochus, son of Nestor, was the first to slay a man of Troy, Echepolus by name, smiting him through the helmet into the forehead. Like a tower he fell, and Elphenor the Eubœan sought to drag him away that he might strip him of his arms. But Agenor smote him with his spear as he stooped, so baring his side to a wound. Dreadful was the fight around his body. Like wolves the Trojans and the Greeks rushed upon each other. And Ajax Telamon slew Simoisius (so they called him, because he was born on the banks of Simois). He fell as a poplar falls, and Antiphon, son of King Priam, aimed at Ajax, but, missing him, slew Leucus, the valiant comrade of Ulysses. And Ulysses, in great anger, stalked through the foremost fighters, brandishing his spear, and the sons of Troy gave way, and when he hurled it he slew Democoön, a son of Priam. Then Hector and the foremost ranks of Troy were borne backward, till Apollo cried from the heights of Pergamos, "On, Trojans! The flesh of these Greeks is not stone or iron, that ye cannot pierce it. Know, too, that the mighty Achilles does not fight to-day." But on the other side Athené urged on the Greeks to battle. Then Peiros the Thracian slew Diores, first striking him to the ground with a huge stone, and then piercing him with his spear; and him in turn Thoas of Ætolia slew, but could not spoil of his arms, so strongly did the men of Thrace defend the body. Then Athené roused Diomed to battle, making a fire shine from his helmet, bright as Orion shines in the vintage time. First there met him two warriors, sons of Dares, priest of Hephæstus, Phegeus and Idæus, the one fighting on foot and the other from his chariot. First Phegeus threw his spear and missed his aim; but Diomed missed not, smiting him through the breast. And Idæus, when he saw his brother fall, fled, Hephæstus saving him, lest the old man should be altogether bereaved. And each of the chiefs slew a foe; but there was none like Diomed, who raged through the battle so furiously that you could not tell with which host he was, whether with the Greeks or with the sons of Troy. Then Pandarus aimed an arrow at him, and smote him in the right shoulder as he was rushing forward, and cried aloud, "On, great-hearted sons of Troy, the bravest of the Greeks is wounded! Soon, methinks, will his strength fail him, unless Apollo has deceived me."

But Diomed cared not for the arrow. Only he leapt down from the chariot and spake to Sthenelus, his charioteer, "Come down and draw this arrow from my shoulder." Then Sthenelus drew it, and the blood spirted out from the wound. And Diomed prayed to Athené, "O goddess, if ever thou hast helped me, be with me now, and grant me to slay this boaster whose arrow has wounded me!" So speaking, he rushed into the ranks of the Trojans, slaying a man at every stroke. Æneas saw him, and thought how he might stay him in his course. So he passed through the host till he found Pandarus. "Pandarus," he said, "where are thy bow and arrows? See how this man deals death through the ranks. Send a shaft at him, first making thy prayer to Zeus."

Then Pandarus answered—

"This man, methinks, is Diomed. The shield and the helmet and the horses are his. And yet I know not whether he is not a god. Some god, at least, stands by him and guards him. But now I sent an arrow at him and smote him on the shoulder, right through the corslet, and thought that I had slain him; but lo! I have harmed him not at all. And now I know not what to do, for here I have no chariot. Eleven, indeed, there are at home, in the house of my father Lycaon, and the old man was earnest with me that I should bring one of them; but I would not, fearing for my horses, lest they should not have provender enough. So I came, trusting in my bow, and lo! it has failed me these two times. Two of the chiefs I have hit, Menelaüs and Diomed, and from each have seen the red blood flow, yet have I not harmed them. Surely, if ever I return safe to my home, I will break this useless bow."

"Nay," said Æneas, "talk not thus. Climb into my chariot, and see what horses we have in Troy. They will carry us safe to the city, even should Diomed prevail against us. But take the rein and the whip, and I will fight; or, if thou wilt, fight thou, and I will drive."

"Nay," said Pandarus, "let the horses have the driver whom they know. It might lose us both, should we turn to flee, and they linger or start aside, missing their master's voice."

So Pandarus mounted the chariot and they drove together against Diomed. And Sthenelus saw them coming, and said to his comrades —"I see two mighty warriors, Lycaon and Æneas. It would be well that we should go back to our chariot."

But Diomed frowned and said, "Talk not of going back. Thou wilt talk in vain to me. As for my chariot, I care not for it. As I am will I go against these men. Both shall not return safe, even if one should escape. But do thou stay my chariot where it is, tying the reins to the rail; and if I slay these men, mount the chariot of Æneas and drive into the host of the Greeks. There are no horses under the sun such as these, for they are of the breed which Zeus himself gave to King Tros."

Meanwhile Pandarus and Æneas were coming near, and Pandarus cast his spear. Right through the shield of Diomed it passed, and reached the corslet, and Pandarus cried—

"Thou art hit in the loin. This, methinks, will lay thee low."

"Nay," said Diomed, "thou hast missed and not hit at all."

And as he spake he threw his spear. Through nose and teeth and tongue it passed, and stood out below the chin. Headlong from the chariot he fell, and his armour clashed about him. Straightway Æneas leapt off with spear and shield to guard the body of his friend, and stood as a lion stands over a carcase. But Diomed lifted a great stone, such as two men of our day could scarcely carry, and cast it. It struck Æneas on the hip, crushing the bone. The hero stooped on his knee, clutching the ground with his hand, and darkness covered his eyes. That hour he had perished, but his mother Aphrodité caught him in her white arms and threw her veil about him. But even so Diomed was loath to let his foe escape, and knowing that the goddess was not of those who mingle in the battle, he rushed on her and wounded her on the wrist, and the blood gushed out—such blood (they call it *ichor*) as flows in the veins of the immortal gods, who eat not the meat and drink not the drink of men. With a loud shriek she dropped her son, but Apollo caught him up and covered him with a dark mist, lest perchance one of the Greeks should spy him and slay him. And still Diomed pursued. Thrice he rushed on, and thrice Apollo pushed back his shining shield; but the fourth time the god cried to him—

"Be wise, son of Tydeus, and give way, nor think to match the gods."

And Diomed gave way, fearing the wrath of the far-shooting bow. But Apollo carried

Æneas out of the battle, and laid him down in his own temple in the citadel of Troy, and there Artemis and Latona healed him of his wound. And all the while the Trojans and the Greeks were fighting, as they thought, about his body, for Apollo had made a likeness of the hero and thrown it down in their midst. Then Sarpedon the Lycian spake to Hector with bitter words—

"Where are thy boasts, Hector? Thou saidst that thou couldst guard thy city, without thy people or thy allies, thou alone, with thy brothers and thy brothers-in-law. But I cannot see even one of them. They go and hide themselves, as dogs before a lion. It is we, your allies, who maintain the battle. I have come from far to help thy people—from Lycia, where I left wife and child and wealth—nor do I shrink from the fight, but thou shouldst do thy part."

And the words stung Hector to the heart. He leapt from his chariot and went through the host, urging them to the battle. And on the other side the Greeks strengthened themselves. But Ares brought back Æneas whole from his wound, and gave him courage and might. Right glad were his comrades to see him, nor did they ask him any question; scant leisure was there for questions that day. Then were done many valiant deeds, nor did any bear himself more bravely than Æneas. Two chieftains of the Greeks he slew, Crethon and Orsilochus, who came from the banks of Alpheüs. Sore vexed was Menelaüs to see them fall, and he rushed to avenge them, Ares urging him on, for he hoped that Æneas would slay him. But Antilochus, Nestor's son, saw him go, and hasted to his side that he might help him. So they went and slew Pylæmenes, King of the Paphlagonians, and Medon, his charioteer. Then Hector rushed to the front, and Ares was by his side. Diomed saw him, and the god also, for his eyes were opened that day, and he fell back a space and cried—

"O my friends! here Hector comes; nor he alone, but Ares is with him in the shape of a mortal man. Let us give place, still keeping our faces to the foe, for men must not fight with gods."

Then drew near to each other Sarpedon the

Lycian and Tlepolemus, the son of Hercules, the one a son and the other a grandson of Zeus. First Tlepolemus spake—

"What art thou doing here, Sarpedon? Surely 'tis a false report that thou art a son of Zeus. The sons of Zeus in the old days were better men than thou art, such as my father Hercules, who came to this city when Laomedon would not give him the horses which he had promised, and brake down the walls and wasted the streets. No help, methinks, wilt thou be to the sons of Troy, slain here by my hands."

But Sarpedon answered, "He indeed spoiled Troy, for Laomedon did him grievous wrong. But thou shalt not fare so, but rather meet with thy death."

Then they both hurled their spears, aiming truly, both of them. For Sarpedon smote Tlepolemus in the neck, piercing it through so that he fell dead, and Tlepolemus smote Sarpedon in the left thigh, driving the spear close to the bone, but slaying him not, his father Zeus warding off the doom of death. And his comrades carried him out of the battle, sorely burdened with the spear, which no one had thought to take out of the wound. And as he was borne along, Hector passed by, and Sarpedon rejoiced to see him, and cried—

"Son of Priam, suffer me not to become a prey to the Greeks; let me at least die in your city, for Lycia I may see no more, nor wife, nor child."

But Hector heeded him not, so eager was he for the battle. So his comrades carried him to the great beech-tree and laid him down, and one of them drew the spear out of his thigh. When it was drawn out he fainted, but the cool north wind blew and revived him, and he breathed again.

But all the while Hector, with Ares at his side, dealt death and destruction through the ranks of the Greeks. Heré and Athené saw him where they sat on the top of Olympus, and were wroth. So they went to Father Zeus, and prayed that it might be lawful to them to stop him in his fury. And Zeus said, "Be it as you will." So they yoked the horses to the chariot of Heré and passed down to earth, the horses flying at every stride over so much space as a man sees who sits upon a cliff and looks across the sea to where it meets the sky. They alighted on the spot where the two rivers Simoïs and Scamander join their streams. There they loosed the horses from the yoke, and then sped like doves to where the bravest of the Greeks stood round King Diomed. There Heré took the shape of Stentor with the lungs of bronze, whose voice was as the voice of fifty men, and cried, "Shame, men of Greece! When Achilles went to the battle, the men of Troy came not beyond the gates, but now they fight far from the city, even by the ships." But Athené went to Diomed where he stood wiping away the blood from the wound where Pandarus had struck him with the arrow. And she spake, "Surely the son of Tydeus is little like to his sire. Small of stature was he, but a keen fighter. But thou—whether it be weariness or fear that keeps thee back I know not—canst scarcely be a true son of Tydeus."

But Diomed answered, " Nay, great goddess, for I know thee who thou art, daughter of Zeus, it is not weariness or fear that keeps me back. 'Tis thy own command that I heed. Thou didst bid me fight with none other of the immortal gods but only with Aphrodité, should she come to the battle. Therefore I give place, for I see Ares lording it through the ranks of war."

"Heed not Ares; drive thy chariot at him, and smite him with the spear. This very morning he promised that he would help the Greeks, and now he hath changed his purpose."

And as she spake she pushed Sthenelus, who drove the chariot, so that he leapt out upon the ground, and she mounted herself and caught the reins and lashed the horses. So the two went together, and they found Ares where he had just slain Periphas the Ætolian. But Athené had donned the helmet of Hades, which whosoever puts on straightway becomes invisible, for she would not that Ares should see her who she was. The god saw Diomed come near, and left Periphas, and cast his spear over the yoke of the chariot, eager to slay the hero. But Athené caught the spear in her hand, and turned it aside, so that it flew vainly through the air. Then Diomed in turn thrust forward his spear, and Athené leant upon it, so that it pierced the loin of Ares, where his girdle was clasped. And Ares shouted with the pain, loud as a host of men, thousands nine or ten, shouts when it joins in battle. And the Greeks and Trojans trembled as they heard. And Diomed saw the god go up to Olympus as a thunder-cloud goes up when the wind of the south blows hot.

But when Ares had departed the Greeks prevailed again, slaying many of the sons of Troy and of their allies. But at last Helenus, the wise seer, spake to Hector and Æneas—

"Cause the army to draw back to the walls, and go through the ranks and give them such strength and courage as ye may. And do thou, Hector, when thou hast so done, pass into the city, and bid thy mother go with the daughters of Troy, and take the costliest robe that she hath, and lay it on the knees of Athené in her temple, vowing therewith to sacrifice twelve heifers, if perchance she may have pity upon us, and keep this Diomed from our walls. Surely there is no Greek so strong as he; we did not fear even Achilles' self so much as we fear this man to-day, so dreadful is he and fierce. Go,

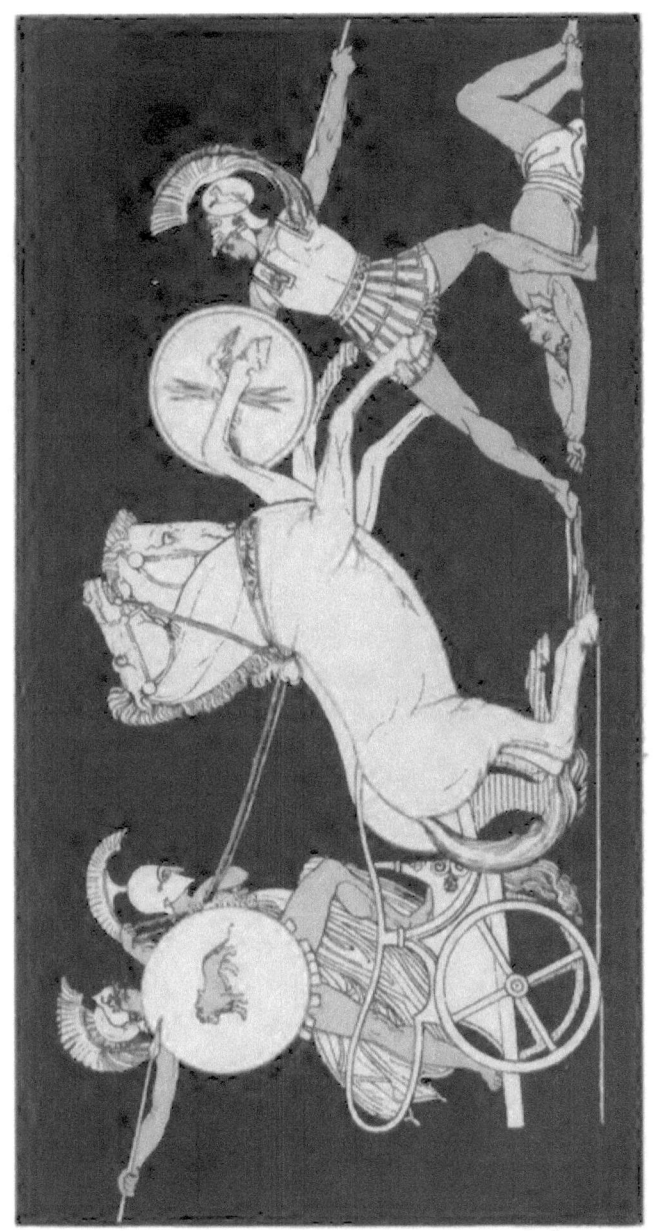

DIOMED CASTING HIS SPEAR AGAINST ARES

and we will make such stand meanwhile as we can."

Then Hector passed through the ranks, bidding them be of good heart, and so departed to the city.

But when he was gone, Glaucus the Lycian and Diomed met in the space between the two hosts. And Diomed said—

"Who art thou that meetest me thus? for never have I seen thee before. If thou art a man, know that luckless are the fathers whose sons meet my spear. But if thou art a god, I will not fight with thee. It fares ill with them that fight with gods."

Then Glaucus answered, "Diomed, why askest thou of my race? The races of men are as the leaves of the forest which the wind blows to the earth, and lo! in the spring they shoot forth again. Yet if thou wouldst know it, hearken to my words. There is a city Ephyra in the land of Argos, where Sisyphus dwelt, who was the craftiest of men; and Sisyphus begat Glaucus, and Glaucus Bellerophon. Now Bellerophon was the fairest and most valiant of men. And Queen Antea accused him falsely to her husband, King Prœtus. Whereupon the king sent him to his father-in-law, who was King of Lycia, and gave him a tablet, whereon were written letters of death, so that the king having read them should cause him to be slain. So Bellerophon came to Lycia. And for nine days the king feasted him, but on the tenth he asked for the tablet. And when he had read it, he sought how he might slay him. For first he sent him to subdue the Chimæra. Now the Chimæra was a marvellous thing, having the forepart of a lion, and the body of a goat, and the tail of a snake. And afterwards he sent him against the Solymi, who are the fiercest warriors of all that dwell on the earth. And his third labour was that he slew the Amazons. And as he was returning the king set an ambush for him, yet harmed him not, for Bellerophon slew all the men that lay in wait for him. Then the king knew him to be a good man and of the race of the gods. Wherefore he kept him, and gave him his daughter to wife, and with her the half of his kingdom; and the Lycians gave him a fair domain of orchard and plough-land. Now Bellerophon had three children—Laodamia, who bare Sarpedon to Zeus; and Isander, whom Ares slew in battle against the Solymi; and Hippolochus, my father, who sent me hither, bidding me ever bear myself bravely, nor shame the race of my fathers."

This Diomed was right glad to hear, and cried, "Nay, but thou art a friend by inheritance. For in former times Œneus, my grandfather, feasted Bellerophon for twenty days, and gave him a belt broidered with purple, and Bellerophon gave him a great cup with two mouths, which indeed I left behind me when I came hither. And now let us two make agreement that we fight not with each other, for there are Trojans enough whom I may slay, and there are Greeks enough for thee. And let us also exchange our armour, that these men may know us to be friends by inheritance."

So they leapt down from their chariots and exchanged their armour. And Zeus took away all wise counsel from the heart of Glaucus, so that he gave golden armour for armour of bronze, the worth of a hundred oxen for the worth of nine.

CHAPTER IV.

HECTOR AND ANDROMACHE.

Hector came into the city by the Scæan gates, and as he went wives and mothers crowded about him, asking how it had fared with their husbands and sons. But he said nought, save to bid them pray; and indeed there was sore news for many, if he had told that which he knew. Then he came to the palace of King Priam, and there he saw Hecuba, his mother, and with her Laodicé, fairest of her daughters. She caught him by the hand and said—

"Why hast thou come from the battle, my son? Do the Greeks press thee hard, and art thou minded to pray to Father Zeus from the citadel? Let me bring thee honey-sweet wine, that thou mayest pour out before him, aye, and that thou mayest drink thyself, and gladden thy heart."

But Hector said, "Give me not wine, my mother, lest thou weaken my knees and make me forget my courage. Nor must I pour out an offering with Zeus thus, with unwashed hands. But do thou gather the mothers of Troy together, and go to the temple of Athené, and take a robe, the one that is the most precious and beautiful in thy stores, and lay it on the knees of the goddess, and pray her to keep this dreadful Diomed from the walls of Troy; and forget not to vow therewith twelve heifers as a sacrifice. As for me, I will go and seek Paris, if perchance he will come with me to the war. Would that the earth might open and swallow him up, for of a truth he is a curse to King Priam and to Troy."

So Queen Hecuba and the mothers of Troy did as Hector had bidden them. But when they laid the robe on the knees of the goddess, she would not hear them.

And Hector went to the house of Paris, where it stood on the citadel, near to his own dwelling and the dwelling of Priam. He found him busy with his arms, and the fair Helen sat near him and gave their tasks to her maidens.

But Hector spake: "Be not wroth, my brother. The people perish about the wall, and the war burns hot round the city, and all for thy sake. Rouse thee, lest it be consumed."

And Paris answered, "Brother, thou hast spoken well. It was not in wrath that I sat here. I was vexed at my sore defeat. But now my wife has urged me to join the battle, and truly it is well, for victory comes now to one and now to another. Wait thou, then, till I don my arms, or if thou wouldst depart, I will overtake thee."

So Hector departed and went to his own home, seeking his wife Andromaché, but found her not, for she was on a tower of the wall with her child and her child's nurse, weeping sore for fear. And Hector spake to the maids—

"Tell me, whither went the white-armed Andromaché; to see some sister-in-law, or to the temple of Athené with the mothers of Troy?"

"Nay," said an aged woman, keeper of the house. "She went to one of the towers of the wall, for she had heard that the Greeks were pressing our people hard. She hasted like as she were mad, and the nurse carried the child."

So Hector ran through the city to the Scæan gates, and there Andromaché spied him, and hasted to meet him—Andromaché, daughter of King Eëtion, of Thebé-under-Placus. And with her was the nurse, bearing the young child on her bosom—Hector's only child, beautiful, headed as a star. His father called him Scamandrius, after the river, but the sons of Troy called him Astyanax, the "City-King," because it was his father who saved the city. Silently he smiled when he saw the child, but Andromaché clasped his hand and wept, and said—

"O Hector, thy courage will bring thee to death. Thou hast no pity on thy wife and child, but sparest not thyself, and all the Greeks will rush on thee and slay thee. It were better for me, losing thee, to die; for I have no comfort but thee. My father is dead, for Achilles slew him in Thebé—slew him but spoiled him not, so much he reverenced him. With his arms he burnt him, and the mountain-nymphs planted poplars about his grave. Seven brethren I had, and lo! they all fell in one day by the hand of the great Achilles. And my mother, she is dead, for when she had been ransomed, Artemis smote her with an arrow in her father's house. But thou art father to me, and mother and brother and husband also. Have pity, then, and stay here upon the wall, lest thou leave me a widow and thy child an orphan. And set the people here in array by this fig-tree, where the city is easiest to be taken; for there come the bravest of the Greeks, Ajax the Greater, and Ajax the Less, and Idomeneus, and the two sons of Atreus, and the son of Tydeus."

But Hector said, "Nay, let these things be my care. I would not that any son or daughter of Troy should see me skulking from the war. And my own heart loathes the thought, and bids me fight in the front. Well I know, indeed, that Priam, and the people of Priam, and holy Troy, will perish. Yet it is not for Troy, or for the people, or even for my father or my mother that I care so much, as for thee in the day when some Greek shall carry thee away

THE MEETING OF HECTOR & ANDROMACHE.

captive, and thou shalt ply the loom or carry the pitcher in the land of Greece. And some one shall say when he sees thee, 'This was Hector's wife, who was the bravest of the sons of Troy.' May the earth cover me before that day!"

Then Hector stretched out his arms to his child. But the child drew back into the bosom of his nurse with a loud cry, fearing the shining bronze and the horse-hair plume which nodded awfully from his helmet top. Then father and mother laughed aloud. And Hector took the helmet from his head and laid it on the ground, and caught his child in his hands, and kissed him and dandled him, praying aloud to Father Zeus and all the gods.

"Grant, Father Zeus and all ye gods, that this child may be as I am, great among the sons of Troy; and may they say some day, when they see him carrying home the bloody spoils from the war, 'A better man than his father, this,' and his mother shall be glad at heart."

Then he gave the child to his mother, and she clasped him to her breast and smiled a tearful smile. And her husband had pity on her, and stroked her with his hand, and spake—

"Be not troubled over much. No man shall slay me against the ordering of fate; but as for fate, that, I trow, no man may escape, be he coward or brave. But go, ply thy tasks, the shuttle and the loom, and give their tasks to thy maidens, and let men take thought for the battle."

Then Hector took up his helmet from the ground, and Andromaché went her way to her home, oft turning back her eyes. And when she was come, she and all her maidens wailed for the living Hector as though he were dead, for she thought that she should never see him any more returning safe from the battle.

And as Hector went his way, Paris came running, clad in shining arms, like to some proud steed which has been fed high in his stall, and now scours the plain with head aloft and mane streaming over his shoulders. And he spake to Hector—

"I have kept thee, I fear, when thou wast in haste, nor came at thy bidding."

But Hector answered, "No man can blame

thy courage, only thou wilfully heldest back from the battle. Therefore do the sons of Troy speak shame of thee. But now let us go to the war."

So they went together out of the gates, and fell upon the host of the Greeks and slew many chiefs of fame, and Glaucus the Lycian went with them.

CHAPTER V.

THE DUEL OF HECTOR AND AJAX.

Now when Athené saw that the Greeks were perishing by the hand of Hector and his companions, it grieved her sore. So she came down from the heights of Olympus, if haply she might help them. And Apollo met her and said—

"Art thou come, Athené, to help the Greeks whom thou lovest? Well, let us stay the battle for this day; hereafter they shall fight till the doom of Troy be accomplished."

But Athené answered, "How shall we stay it?"

And Apollo said, "We will set on Hector to challenge the bravest of the Greeks to fight with him, man to man."

So they two put the matter into the mind of Helenus the seer. Then Helenus went near to Hector—

"Listen to me, for I am thy brother. Cause the rest of the sons of Troy and of the Greeks to sit down, and do thou challenge the bravest of the Greeks to fight with thee, man to man. And be sure thou shalt not fall in the battle, for the will of the immortal gods is so."

Then Hector greatly rejoiced, and passed to the front of the army, holding his spear by the middle, and kept back the sons of Troy; and King Agamemnon did likewise with his own people. Then Hector spake—

"Hear me, sons of Troy, and ye men of Greece. The covenant that we made one with another hath been broken, for Zeus would have it so, purposing evil to both, till either you shall take our high-walled city or we shall conquer you by your ships. But let one of you who call yourselves champions of the Greeks come forth and fight with me, man to man. And let it be so that if he vanquish me he shall spoil me of my arms but give my body to my people, that they may burn it with fire; and if I vanquish him, I will spoil him of his arms but give his body to the Greeks, that they may bury him and raise a great mound above him by the broad salt river of Hellespont. And so men of after days shall see it, sailing by, and say, 'This is the tomb of the bravest of the Greeks, whom Hector slew.' So shall my name live for ever."

But all the Greeks kept silence, fearing to meet him in battle, but shamed to hold back. Then at last Menelaüs leapt forward and spake—

"Surely now ye are women and not men. Foul shame it were should there be no man to stand up against this Hector. Lo! I will fight with him my own self, for the issues of battle are with the immortal gods."

So he spake in his rage rashly, courting death, for Hector was much stronger than he. Then King Agamemnon answered—

"Nay, but this is folly, my brother. Seek not in thy anger to fight with one that is stronger than thou; for as for this Hector, even Achilles was loth to meet him. Sit thou down among thy comrades, and the Greeks will find some champion who shall fight with him."

And Menelaüs hearkened to his brother's words, and sat down. Then Nestor rose in the midst and spake—

"Woe is me to-day for Greece! How would the old Peleus grieve to hear such a tale! Well I remember how he rejoiced when I told him of the house and lineage of all the chieftains of the Greeks, and now he would hear that they cower before Hector, and are sore afraid when he calls them to the battle. Surely he would pray this day that he might die! Oh that I were such as I was in the old days, when the men of Pylos fought with the Arcadians by the stream of Iardanus! Now the leader of the Arcadians was Ereuthalion, and he wore the arms of Areïthous, whom men called 'Areïthous of the club,' because he fought not with bow or spear, but with a club of iron. Him Lycurgus slew, not by might but by craft, taking him in a narrow place where his club of iron availed him not, and smiting him with his spear. He slew him, and took his arms. And when Lycurgus grew old he gave the arms to Ereuthalion to wear. So Ereuthalion wore them, and challenged the men of Pylos to fight with him. But they feared him. Only I, who was the youngest of all, stood forth, and Athené gave me glory that day, for I slew him, though he was the strongest and tallest among the sons of men. Would that I were such to-day! Right soon would I meet this mighty Hector."

Then rose up nine chiefs of fame. First of all, King Agamemnon, lord of many nations, and next to him Diomed, son of Tydeus, and Ajax the Greater and Ajax the Less, and then Idomeneus and Meriones, who was his companion in arms, and Eurypylus, and Thoas, son of Andræmon, and the wise Ulysses.

Then Nestor said, "Let us cast lots who shall do battle with the mighty Hector."

So they threw the lots into the helmet of King Agamemnon, a lot for each. And the people prayed, "Grant, ye gods, that the lot of Ajax the Greater may leap forth, or the lot of Diomed, or the lot of King Agamemnon." Then Nestor shook the lots in the helmet, and the one which they most wished leapt forth. For the herald took it through the ranks and showed it to the chiefs, but none knew it for his own till he came to where Ajax the Greater stood among his comrades. But Ajax had marked it with his mark, and put forth his hand for it, and claimed it, right glad at heart. On the ground by his feet he threw it, and said—

"Mine is the lot, my friends, and right glad I am, for I think that I shall prevail over the mighty Hector. But come, let me don my arms; and pray ye to Zeus, but silently, lest the Trojans hear, or aloud, if ye will, for no fear have we. Not by force or craft shall any one vanquish me, for not such are the men whom Salamis breeds."

So he armed himself and moved forwards, dreadful as Ares, smiling with grim face. With mighty strides he came, brandishing his long-shafted spear. And all the Greeks were glad to behold him, but the knees of the Trojans were loosened with fear, and great Hector's heart beat fast; but he trembled not, nor gave place, seeing that he had himself called him to battle. So Ajax came near, holding before the great shield, like a wall, which Tychius, best of craftsmen, had made for him. Seven folds of bull's hide it had, and an eighth of bronze. Threateningly he spake—

"Now shalt thou know, Hector, what manner of men there are yet among our chiefs, though Achilles the lion-hearted is far away, sitting idly in his tent, in great wrath with King Agamemnon. Do thou, then, begin the battle."

"Speak not to me, Zeus-descended Ajax," said

Hector, "as though I were a woman or a child, knowing nothing of war. Well I know all the arts of battle, to ply my shield this way and that, to guide my car through the tumult of steeds, and to stand fighting hand to hand. But I would not smite so stout a foe by stealth, but openly, if it so befall."

And as he spake he hurled his long-shafted spear, and smote the great shield on the rim of the eighth fold, that was of bronze. Through six folds it passed, but in the seventh it was stayed. Then Ajax hurled his spear, striking Hector's shield. Through shield it passed and corslet, and cut the tunic close against the loin; but Hector shrank away and escaped the doom of death. Then, each with a fresh spear, they rushed together like lions or wild boars of the wood. First Hector smote the middle of the shield of Ajax, but pierced it not, for the spear-point was bent back; then Ajax, with a great bound, drove his spear at Hector's shield and pierced it, forcing him back, and grazing his neck so that the black blood welled out. Yet did not Hector cease from the combat. A great stone and rough he caught up from the ground, and hurled it at the boss of the sevenfold shield. Loud rang the bronze, but the shield brake not. Then Ajax took a stone heavier by far, and threw it with all his might. It brake the shield of Hector, and bore him backwards, so that he fell at length with his shield above him. But Apollo raised him up. Then did both draw their swords; but ere they could join in close battle came the heralds, and held their sceptres between them, and Idæus, the herald of Troy, spake—

"Fight no more, my sons; Zeus loves you both; and ye are both mighty warriors. That we all know right well. But now the night bids you cease, and it is well to heed its bidding."

Then said Ajax, "Nay, Idæus, but it is for Hector to speak, for he called the bravest of the Greeks to battle. And as he wills it, so will I."

And Hector said, "O Ajax, the gods have given thee stature and strength and skill, nor is there any better warrior among the Greeks. Let us cease then from the battle; we may yet meet again, till the gods give the victory to me or thee. And now let us give gifts the one to the other, so that Trojans and Greeks may say —Hector and Ajax met in fierce fight and parted in friendship."

So Hector gave to Ajax a silver-studded sword with the scabbard and the sword-belt, and Ajax gave to Hector a buckler splendid with purple. So they parted. Right glad were the sons of Troy when they saw Hector returning safe. Glad also were the Greeks, as they led Ajax rejoicing in his victory to King Agamemnon. Whereupon the king called the chiefs to banquet together, and bade slay an ox of five years old, and Ajax he honoured most of all, giving him the chine. And when the feast was ended Nestor said—

"It were well that we should cease awhile from war and burn the dead, for many, in truth, are fallen. And we will build a great wall and dig a trench about it, and we will make gates, wide that a chariot may pass through, so that our ships may be safe, if the sons of Troy should press us hard."

But the next morning came a herald from Troy to the chiefs as they sat in council by the ship of King Agamemnon, and said—

HECTOR & AJAX SEPERATED BY THE HERALDS.

"This is the word of Priam and the men of Troy: Paris will give back all the treasures of the fair Helen, and many more besides; but the fair Helen herself he will not give. But if this please you not, grant us a truce, that we may bury our dead."

Then Diomed spake, "Nay, we will not take the fair Helen's self, for a man may know, even though he be a fool, that the doom of Troy is come."

And King Agamemnon said, "Herald, thou hast heard the word of the Greeks, but as for the truce, be it as you will."

So the next day they burnt their dead, and the Greeks made a wall with gates and dug a trench about it. And when it was finished, even at sunset, they made ready a meal, and lo! there came ships from Lemnos bringing wine, and Greeks bought thereof, some with bronze, and some with iron, and some with shields of ox hide. All night they feasted right joyously. The sons of Troy also feasted in their city. But the dreadful thunder rolled through the night, for Zeus was counselling evil against them.

CHAPTER VI.

THE ADVENTURE OF ULYSSES AND DIOMED.

ON the morrow they set the battle in array against each other, and many valiant deeds were done that day which it were long to tell. Till midday, indeed, neither this side prevailed nor that. But at noon Father Zeus sent his terror on the Greeks, and they fled. Then old Nestor came near to be taken by the Trojans, for Paris had slain one of the horses of his chariot with an arrow. Only Diomed came near and helped him, making him mount his own chariot, and slaying with his spear the charioteer of Hector. And more he would have done, but Zeus sent down great lightning from heaven, striking the ground in front of the chariot.

Then Nestor said, "Let us flee, King Diomed, for Zeus denies us victory, and a man may not fight with Zeus."

And he constrained him so that he turned

his horses and fled. But Hector cried after him, "Art *thou* the man to whom the Greeks give high place in the feast, and plenteous cups of wine? Not so will they honour thee hereafter. Run, girl! run, coward! Shalt *thou* climb our walls and carry away our daughters in thy ships?"

Then Diomed was very wroth, doubting whether to flee or to turn; but when he turned Zeus thundered from on high, making him afraid. And Hector bade the hosts of Troy be of good courage, for that Zeus was with them, and called to his horses—

"Come now, Bayard, and Whitefoot, and Flame of Fire, and Brilliant; forget not how the fair Andromaché has cared for you; aye, even before me, who am her husband. Carry me fast, that I may win old Nestor's shield, which men say is all of gold, and strip from the shoulders of Diomed the breastplate which Hephæstus wrought."

And Hector that hour would have stormed the wall and burnt the ships, but King Agamemnon prayed aloud to Zeus, and Zeus heard him and sent a sign, an eagle which dropped a kid out of his claws. Then the

Greeks took heart again, and among them Teucer wrought great deeds, shooting his arrows from under the shield of Ajax, his brother. Many Trojans he slew, and twice he sent a shaft at Hector: with the first he slew Gorgythion, Hector's brother, and with the second Cebriones, his charioteer. Then Hector in great anger rushed at Teucer, and Teucer fitted an arrow to the string to shoot at him; but ere he could loose it, Hector smote him with a great stone and brake the string, and numbed the hand at the wrist. Then he dropped the bow, and his comrades carried him away groaning to the ships. Nor after that did the Greeks hold up at all in the battle. Glad were they to see the darkness come; but the Trojans liked it not, for they had thought to make a full end that day of their enemies. Then Hector gathered his people together on the river bank, where there was a space clear of dead bodies, and bade them be of good cheer and make merry, for that on the morrow they would utterly destroy the Greeks. So all that night they lay encamped on the plain, a thousand watch-fires, and round each watch-fire fifty men; and the horses, standing by the chariots, and eating white barley and spelt, waited for the dawn.

Meanwhile King Agamemnon held a council of the chiefs. And first he would have had them flee to their homes, for Troy, he said, they would never take.

Then out spake King Diomed: "Be not angry, great king, if I speak plainly, as befits him who would give good counsel. Thou didst call me coward once, nor did ever man so before; but I see that Zeus, who gave thee a great throne among men, did not give thee courage. Go, if it be thy wish, and thy ships with thee, but the other men of Greece will stay; nay, though all depart, yet will I and Sthenelus abide till the doom of Troy be come, for of a surety it was by the bidding of the gods that we came hither."

And all the chiefs said that it was well. Then, at the bidding of Nestor, they made captains of the watch who should guard the wall. And after that King Agamemnon made a feast, and, the feast ended, Nestor counselled that he should make peace with Achilles, which Agamemnon himself was minded to do. So they chose

Phœnix, who had been the teacher of Achilles in the old days, and Ajax the Greater, and Ulysses; and these three went to Achilles and told him all that King Agamemnon would give if he would only cease from his wrath: seven kettles of brass, three-footed, that had never felt the fire; and ten talents of gold, and twenty caldrons, and twelve horses which should win great riches for their master by their running; and seven women of Lesbos, skilled in all the works of the loom; and, chief of all, Briseïs, for whom all this trouble had been; and when Troy should be taken, much spoil besides, and when they should have returned home, one of his daughters to wife, and with her seven cities by the sea. But Achilles would have none of these things, but kept his anger still; for the gods would have it so, till all the doom should be accomplished. So the three returned to King Agamemnon, and told him how they had fared; and he was sorely troubled, and the same night he called together again all the wisest of the chiefs. First they went round to the guards, and found them all watchful, and then they took counsel in an open space beyond the trench.

And Nestor rose and said, "Is there now a man who will go among the sons of Troy and see what they are minded to do? Great honour will he win, and gifts withal."

Then Diomed said, "I am ready to go, but I would fain have some one with me. To have a companion gives comfort and courage, and, indeed, two wits are better than one to take counsel and to foresee."

And many were willing to go: Ajax the Greater, and Ajax the Less, and Meriones, and Antilochus, old Nestor's son (and no one indeed wished it more than he), and Menelaüs and Ulysses.

But Agamemnon said, "Choose the best man, O Diomed, and regard not the birth or rank of any." This he said, fearing for his brother Menelaüs.

And Diomed answered, "Nay, but if I may choose, whom should I choose rather than the wise Ulysses? Brave is he, and prudent, and Athené loves him well."

But Ulysses said, "Praise me not overmuch, nor blame me. Only let us go, for the night is far spent."

So these two armed themselves. Diomed took a two-edged sword and a shield, and a helmet without a crest, and Ulysses a bow and a quiver and a sword, and a helmet of hide with the white teeth of a wild boar about it. Then both prayed to Athené that she would help them, and after that they went through the darkness like to two lions, trampling over dead bodies and arms and blood.

But Hector meanwhile was thinking on the same things, for he called the chiefs to a council and said, "Who now will go and spy among the Greeks, and see what they purpose to do on the morrow, and whether they are keeping watch through the night. A goodly reward shall he have, even a chariot and horses, the best that there are in the camp of the Greeks."

Then stood up a certain Dolon, the son of the herald Eumedes. Ill-favoured was he, but a swift runner. He said—

"I will go, Hector; but come, lift up thy sceptre, and swear to me that thou wilt give me the chariot and the horses of Achilles."

So Hector sware to him. And Dolon took his bow, and a helmet of grisly wolf-skin, and a sharp spear, and went his way in haste. But Ulysses saw him, and said—

"Here cometh a man, Diomed, but whether he be a spy or a spoiler of the dead I know not. Let him pass by a space, that we may take him. Only let him not turn back to the city."

So they lay down among the dead, a little out of the way, and Dolon passed by them unknowing; but when he had gone a little space they ran upon him. For a while he stood hearkening to their steps, for he thought that Hector had sent comrades to call him back. But when they were a spear's throw from him, or less, he knew them for foes, and fled. And just as two dogs follow a fawn or a hare, so they two ran, pursuing Dolon. And when he had well-nigh reached the trench, for they kept him that he should not turn back to the city, Diomed rushed forward and cried—

"Stay, or I will slay thee with my spear."

And he threw the spear, and smote not the man indeed, for that he wished not, but made it pass over his shoulder, so that it stood in the ground before him. Then Dolon stood trembling and pale, and with teeth chattering with fear. And the two heroes, breathing hard, came up and laid hands on him. And he said, weeping—

"Hold me to ransom; much gold and bronze and iron will my father give, if he hear that I am a prisoner at the ships."

Then said the wise Ulysses, "Be of good cheer, and think not of death. But tell us truly, why wast thou coming hither through the darkness? To spoil the dead, or, at Hector's bidding, to spy out our affairs at the ships, or on some errand of thine own?"

And Dolon answered, "Hector persuaded me, promising to give me the horses and chariot of Achilles, and he bade me go and spy out what ye purposed to do on the morrow, and whether ye were keeping watch in the night."

And Ulysses smiled and said, "Surely it was a great reward that thy soul desired. The horses of Achilles are grievous for any man to drive, save for him that is born of a goddess. But tell me, where is Hector, and where are the watches of the sons of Troy?"

Then Dolon answered, "Hector holds council with the chiefs by the tomb of Ilus. But as for the army, there are no watches set, save only where be the Trojans themselves. But as for the allies, they sleep secure, and trust to the Trojans to watch for them, seeing that they have not wives or children near."

Then Ulysses asked, "Do they sleep, then, among the Trojans, or apart?"

"Next to the sea," said Dolon, "are the men of Caria and Pæonia, and close to these the men of Lycia and Mysia and Phrygia. But if ye wish to enter the camp, lo! apart from all are some new-comers, Thracians, with Rhesus, their king. Never have I seen horses so fair and tall as his. Whiter are they than snow, and swifter than the winds. But do ye now send me to the ships, or, if ye will, bind me and leave me here."

But Diomed said, "Think not to escape, Dolon, though thy news is good; for then wouldst thou come again to spy out our camp or to fight. But if I slay thee, thou wilt trouble the Greeks no more."

So he slew him, and took from him his arms, hanging them on a tamarisk tree, and made a mark with reeds and tamarisk boughs, that they might know the place as they came back. So they went on across the plain and came to where the men of Thrace lay sleeping, and by each man were his arms in fair array, and his horses; but in the midst lay King Rhesus, with his horses tethered to the chariot-rail. Then Diomed began to slay. As a lion rushes on a flock, so rushed he on the men of Thrace. Twelve he slew, and as he slew them Ulysses dragged them out of the way, that there might be a clear road for the horses, lest they should start back, fearing the dead bodies, for they were not used to war. And the thirteenth was King Rhesus himself, who panted in his sleep, for an evil dream was on him. And meanwhile Ulysses drove the horses out of the encampment, smiting them with his bow, for he had not thought to take the whip out of the chariot. Then he whistled, making a sign to Diomed that he should come, for Diomed lingered, doubting whether he might not slay yet more. But Athené whispered in his ear—

"Think of thy return, lest haply some god rouse the Trojans against thee."

And, indeed, Apollo was even then rousing them. For Hippocoön, cousin to King Rhesus,

DIOMED & ULYSSES, RETURNING WITH THE SPOILS OF RHESUS.

awoke, and seeing the place of the horses empty and his comrades slain, groaned aloud, and called to the king, and the Trojans were roused, and flocked together with tumult and shouting. But Diomed and Ulysses meanwhile had mounted the horses, and were riding to the ships. Glad were their comrades to see them safe returned, and praised them much for all that they had done.

CHAPTER VII.

THE WOUNDING OF THE CHIEFS.

THE next day the battle was set in array as before. And all the morning the armies fought without advantage to the one or the other; but at noon, at the hour when one who cuts wood upon the hills sits down to his meal, the Greeks prevailed and drove back the sons of Troy. Nor was there one of all the chiefs who fought so bravely as King Agamemnon. Many valiant men he slew, and among them the two sons of Antimachus. These, indeed, he took alive in their chariot, for they had dropped the reins and stood helpless before him, crying out that he should spare them and take ransom, for that Antimachus their father had much gold and bronze and iron in his house, and would gladly buy them back alive. Now Antimachus had taken a bribe from Prince Paris, and had given counsel to the Trojans that they should not give back the fair Helen. So when King Agamemnon heard them, he said, " Nay, but if ye be sons of Antimachus, who counselled the men of Troy that they should slay Menelaüs when he came an ambassador to their city, ye shall die for your father's sin." So he slew them both, and leaving them, he still rushed on, driving back the Trojans even to the walls of their city. Nor did Hector himself dare to meet him, for Zeus had sent him a message, saying that he should hold himself back till King Agamemnon should chance to be wounded. And, indeed, this chance happened presently, for the king had slain Iphidamas, son to Antenor, and Coön, his brother, the eldest born, was very wroth to see it. So standing sideways he aimed with his spear, Agamemnon not knowing, and smote the king in the hand near the wrist. Then he seized the body of his brother, and shouted to his comrades that they should help him ; but Agamemnon dealt him a deadly blow underneath his shield. So he fell ; and for a while, while the wound was warm, the king fought as before ; but when it grew cold and stiff, great pain came upon him, and he leapt into his chariot and bade the charioteer drive him to the ships, for that he could fight no more.

Then again the battle went for the Trojans, though Diomed and Ulysses, who fought very valiantly, stayed it awhile, Diomed coming very near to slay Hector. But Paris, who was in hiding behind the pillar on the tomb of Ilus, drew his bow, and smote him with an arrow through the ankle of the right foot. Loud he boasted of his aim. "Only," he said, "I would that I had pierced thee in the loin; then hadst thou troubled the sons of Troy no more."

But Diomed answered, "Small good were thy bow to thee, cowardly archer, if thou shouldst dare to meet me face to face. And as for this graze on my foot, I care no more than if a woman or child had smitten me. Not such the wounds I deal; as for those that meet my spear in the battle, I trow that they are dearer to the fowls of the air than to women in the chamber."

Then Ulysses stood before him while he drew the arrow out of his foot. Grievous was the smart of the wound, for all his brave words. Wherefore he leapt into his chariot, and bade drive in haste to the ships. So Ulysses was left alone, and the Trojans came about him as men with dogs come about a wild boar who stands at bay gnashing his white teeth. Fiercely he stood at bay, and slew five chiefs of fame. But one of them, Socus by name, before he fell, wounded him on the side, scraping the flesh from the ribs. High spurted the blood from the wound, and the Trojans shouted to see it. Then Ulysses shouted for help; three times he shouted, and Menelaüs heard him, and called to Ajax that it was the voice of Ulysses, and that they should help him. So they went together and made head awhile against the Trojans. But soon Paris wounded with an arrow another brave chieftain, even the physician Machaon. Then Ajax himself was affrighted and gave way, but slowly, and sore against his will. Just so a lion is driven off from a herd of oxen by dogs and men. Loath he is to go, so hungry is he, but the spears and the burning torches affright him. So Ajax gave way. Now he would turn and face the sons of Troy, and now he would flee, and they sought how to slay him, but harmed him not. Then once more Paris loosed his bow and wounded a chief, Eurypylus, striking him on the right thigh. So the battle went sorely against the Greeks.

Now Achilles was standing on the stern of his ship, looking at the war, and he saw Nestor carrying Machaon in his chariot to the ships. Then he called to Patroclus, and Patroclus, who was in the tent, came forth; but it was an evil hour for him. Then said Achilles—

"Now will the Greeks soon come, methinks, praying for help, for their need is sore. But go and see who is this whom Nestor is taking to the ships. His shoulders are the shoulders of Machaon, but I saw not his face, so swift the horses passed me by."

Then Patroclus ran. And as he stood in the tent door old Nestor saw him, and went and took him by the hand, and would have had him sit down. But Patroclus would not, saying—

"Stay me not. I came but to see who is this that thou hast brought wounded from the battle. And now I see that it is Machaon. Therefore I will return, for thou knowest what manner of man is Achilles, that he is hasty and swift to blame."

Then said Nestor, " But what cares Achilles for the Greeks ? or why does he ask who are wounded ? But, O Patroclus, dost thou mind the day when I and Ulysses came to the house of Peleus, and how that thy father Menætius was there, and how we feasted in the hall ; and when the feast was finished told our errand, for we were gathering the heroes for the war against the sons of Troy ? Right willing were ye two to come, and many counsels did the old men give you. Then to Achilles Peleus said that he should always be foremost in the host, but to thee thy father Menætius spake, ' Achilles is nobler born than thou, and stronger far; but thou art older. Do thou therefore counsel him well, when there is need.' But this thou forgettest, Patroclus. Hear, then, what I say. It may be that Achilles will not go forth to the battle. But let him send thee forth, and the Myrmidons with thee, and let him put his arms upon thee, so that the sons of Troy be affrighted, thinking that he is in the battle, and we shall have breathing space."

Then Patroclus turned to run to Achilles, but as he ran he met Eurypylus, who spake to him—

"Small hope is there now for the Greeks, seeing that all their bravest chiefs lie wounded at the ships. But do thou help me, for thou knowest all the secrets of healing, seeing that the wise Chiron himself taught thee."

Then Patroclus answered, "I am even now on my way to tell these things to Achilles, but thee I may not leave in thy trouble."

So he took him to his tent, and cut out the arrow from his thigh, washing the wound with water, and putting on it a bitter healing root, so that the pain was stayed and the blood stanched.

CHAPTER VIII.

THE BATTLE AT THE WALL.

Now by this time the Trojans were close upon the trench. But the horses stood on the brink, fearing to leap it, for it was broad and deep, and the Greeks had put great stakes therein. Thus said Polydamas—

"Surely, Hector, this is madness that we strive to cross the trench in our chariots, for it is broad and deep, and there are great stakes therein. Look, too, at this: even if we should be able to cross it, how will the matter stand? If indeed it be the pleasure of Zeus that the Greeks should perish utterly—it will be well. But if they turn upon us and pursue us, driving us back from the ships, then shall we not be able to return. Wherefore let us leave our chariots here upon the brink, and go on foot against the wall."

So they went in five companies, of whom Hector led that which was bravest and largest, and with him were Polydamas and Cebriones. And the next Paris commanded. And of the third Helenus and Deïphobus were leaders, and with them was Asius, the son of Hyrtacus, from Arisbé. And the fourth followed Æneas, the valiant son of Anchises. But of the allies Sarpedon was the leader, and with him were Glaucus and Asteropæus. And in each company they joined shield to shield, and so went against the Greeks. Nor was there one of them but hearkened to the counsel of Polydamas when he bade them leave their chariots by the trench, save Asius only. But Asius drove his chariot right up to that gate which was on the left hand in the wall. Now the gates chanced to be open, for the warders had opened them, if so any of the Greeks that fled might save themselves within them. Now the warders were two mighty heroes of the race of the Lapithæ, Polypœtes and Leonteus; and these, when they saw Asius and his company coming, went without and stood in front of the gates, just as two wild boars stand at bay against a crowd of men and dogs. And all the while they that stood on the wall threw heavy stones which fell, thick as the snow-flakes fall in the winter, on the men of Troy, and loud rang the helmets and the shields. And many fell wounded to the death, nor could Asius, for all his fury, win his way into the walls. But where, at another of the gates, Hector led the way, there appeared a strange marvel in the skies, for an eagle was bearing in his claws a great snake, which it had taken as a prey. But the snake fought fiercely for its life, and writhed itself about, even till it bit the eagle on the breast. Whereupon the eagle dropped it into the midst of the host, and fled with a loud cry. Then Polydamas, the wise counsellor, came near to Hector and said—

"Now it will be well that we should not follow these Greeks to their ships. For I take that this marvel that we have seen is a sign to us. For as this eagle had caught in his claws a snake, but held it not, dropping it before it could bear it to her young, so shall it fare with us. For we shall drive the Greeks to their ships, but shall not subdue them but shall return in disorder by the way that we came, leaving full many of our comrades behind us."

But Hector frowned and answered, "Nay, but this is ill counsel, Polydamas. For if thou sayest this from thy heart, surely the gods have changed thy wisdom into foolishness. Dost thou bid me forget the command of Zeus the Thunderer, and take heed to birds, how they fly? Little care I whether they go to the east or to the west, to the right or to the left. Surely there is but one sign for a brave man, that he be fighting for his fatherland. Wherefore take thou heed; for if thou holdest back from the war, or holdest back any other, lo! I will smite thee with my spear."

Then he sprang forward, and the men of Troy followed him with a shout. And Zeus sent down from Ida a great blast of wind which bore the dust of the plain straight to the ships, troubling the hearts of the Greeks. Then the Trojans sought to drag down the battlements from the wall, and to wrench up the posts which had been set to strengthen it. Nor did the Greeks give way, but they joined shield to shield and fought for the wall. And foremost among them were Ajax the Greater and Ajax the Less. Just as the snow falls in mid-winter, when the winds are hushed, and the mountain-tops are covered, and the plains and the dwellings of men and the very shores of the sea, up to the waves' edge, so thickly fell the stones which the Greeks showered from the wall against the men of Troy, and which these again threw upon the Greeks. But still Hector and his men availed not to break through the gate. But at the last Zeus stirred up the heart of his own son, Sarpedon. Holding his shield before him he went, and he shook in either hand a spear. As goes a lion, when hunger presses him sore, against a stall of oxen or a sheepfold, and cares not though he find men and dogs keeping watch against him, so Sarpedon went against the wall. And first he spake to stout Glaucus, his comrade—

"Tell me, Glaucus, why is it that men honour us at home with the chief rooms at feasts, and with fat portions of flesh and with sweet wine, and that we have a great domain of orchard and plough land by the banks of Xanthus? Surely it is that we may fight in the front rank.

Then shall some one who may behold us say, 'Of a truth these are honourable men, these princes of Lycia, and not without good right do they eat the fat and drink the sweet, for they fight ever in the front.' Now, indeed, if we might live for ever, nor know old age nor death, neither would I fight among the first, nor would I bid thee arm thyself for the battle. But seeing that there are ten thousand fates about us which no man may avoid, let us see whether we shall win glory from another, or another shall take it from us."

And Glaucus listened to his words and charged at his side, and the great host of the Lycians followed them. Sore dismayed was Menestheus the Athenian when he saw them. All along the wall of the Greeks he looked, spying out for help; and he saw Ajax the Greater and Ajax the Less, and with them Teucer, who had just come forth from his tent. Close to him they were, but it was of no avail to shout, so loud was the clash and din of arms, of shield and helmets, and the thundering at the gates, for each one of these did the men of Troy assail.

Wherefore he called to him Thoas, the herald,

and said, "Run, Thoas, and call Ajax hither—both of the name if that may be—for the end is close upon us in this place, so mightily press on the chiefs of the Lycians, who were ever fiery fighters. But if there is trouble there also, let at the least Ajax the Greater come, and with him Teucer of the bow."

Then the herald ran, and said as he had been bidden.

And Ajax Telamon spake to the son of Oïleus: "Stand thou here with Lycomedes and stay the enemy. But I will go thither, and come again when I have finished my work."

So he went, and Teucer his brother went with him, with Pandion carrying his bow. And even as they went the Lycians came up like a tempest on the wall. But Ajax slew Epicles, a comrade of Sarpedon, smiting him on the head with a mighty stone, and crushing all the bones of his head. And Teucer smote Glaucus on the shoulder and wounded him sore. Silently did Glaucus leap down from the wall, for he would not that any of the Greeks should see that he was wounded. But Sarpedon saw that he had departed, and it grieved him.

Nevertheless, he ceased not from the battle, but first slew Alcmaon, the son of Mestor, and next caught one of the battlements in his hands and dragged it down. So the wall was laid open, and a way was made for the Trojans to enter. Then did both Ajax and Teucer aim at him together. And Teucer smote the strap of the shield, but harmed him not, and Ajax drove his spear through his shield and stayed him, so that he fell back a space from the battlement, yet would not cease from the fight. Loud he shouted to the Lycians that they should follow him, and they came crowding about their king. Then fierce and long was the fight, for the Lycians could not break down the wall of the Greeks and make a way to the ships, and the Greeks could not drive away the Lycians from the wall where they stood. Just so two men contend for the boundary in some common field. Small is the space, and they stand close together. So close stood the Lycians and the Greeks, on this side of the battlement, and on that, and all the wall was red with blood. But not to Sarpedon and the men of Lycia, but to Hector, did Zeus give the glory that day. Now, in front of the gate there lay a great stone, broad at the base and sharp at the top. Scarce could two men of the strongest, such as are men in these days, move it with levers on to a waggon; but Hector lifted it easily, easily as a shepherd carries in one hand the fleece of a sheep. Two folding doors there were in the gates, held by bolts and a key, and at these he hurled the great stone, planting his feet apart, that his aim might be the surer and stronger. With a mighty crash it came against the gates, and the bolts held not against it, and the hinges were broken, so that the folding doors flew back. Then Hector leapt into the space, holding a spear in either hand, and his eyes flashed as fire. And the men of Troy came after him, some mounting the wall, and some pouring through the gates.

CHAPTER IX.

THE BATTLE AT THE SHIPS.

Now Poseidon was watching the battle from the wooded height of Samothrace, whence he could see Ida and Troy and the ships. And he pitied the Greeks when he saw how they fled before Hector, and purposed in his heart to help them. So he left the height of Samothrace, and came with four strides to Ægæ, where his palace was in the depths of the sea. There he harnessed the horses to his chariot and rode, passing over the waves, and the great beasts of the sea gambolled about him as he went, knowing their king. But when he came to the camp of the Greeks, he took upon him the shape of Calchas, the herald, and went through the host strengthening the heroes for the battle—Ajax the Greater, and Ajax the Less, and others also—so that they turned their faces again to the enemy. But not the less did the men of Troy press on, Hector leading the way.

Then first of all Teucer slew a Trojan, Imbrius by name, wounding him under the ear. He fell as some tall poplar falls which a woodman fells with axe of bronze. Then Teucer rushed to seize his arms, but Hector cast his spear. Teucer it struck not, missing him by a little, but Amphimachus it smote on the breast so that he fell dead. Then Hector seized the dead man's helmet, seeking to drag the body among the sons of Troy. But Ajax stretched forth his great spear against him, and struck the boss of his shield mightily, driving him backwards, so that he loosed hold of the helmet of Amphimachus. And him his comrades bore to the rear of the host, and the body of Imbrius also they carried off. Then did Idomeneus the Cretan, son of Minos, the wise judge, perform many valiant deeds, going to the left-hand of the battle-line, for he said—

"The Greeks have stay enough where the great Ajax is. No man that eats bread is better than he; no, not Achilles' self, were the two to stand man to man, but Achilles indeed is swifter of foot."

And first of all he slew Othryoneus, who had but newly come, hearing the fame of the war. For Cassandra's sake he had come, that he might have her to wife, vowing that he would drive the Greeks from Troy, and Priam had promised him the maiden. But now Idomeneus slew him, and cried over him—

"This was a great thing that thou didst promise to Priam, for which he was to give thee his daughter. Thou shouldst have come to us, and we would have given thee the fairest of the daughters of Agamemnon, bringing her from Argos, if thou wouldst have engaged to help us to take this city of Troy. But come now with me to the ships, that we may treat about this marriage: thou wilt find that we have open hands."

So he spake, mocking the dead. Then King Asius charged, coming on foot with his chariot behind him. But ere he could throw his spear, Idomeneus smote him that he fell, as falls an oak, or an alder, or a pine, which men fell upon the hills. And the driver of his chariot stood dismayed, nor thought to turn his horses and flee, so that Antilochus, the son of Nestor, struck him down, and took the chariot and horses for his own. Then Deïphobus in great wrath came near to Idomeneus, and would have slain him with a spear, but could not, for he covered himself with his shield, and the spear passed over his head. Yet did it not fly in vain, for it lighted on Hypsenor, striking him on the right side. And as he fell, Deïphobus cried aloud—

"Now is Asius avenged; and though he go down to that strong porter who keeps the gates of hell, yet will he be glad, for I have sent him a companion."

But scarce had he spoken when Idomeneus the Cretan slew another of the chiefs of Troy, Alcathoüs, son-in-law of old Anchises. And having slain him he cried—

"Small reason hast thou to boast, Deïphobus for we have slain three for one. But come thou and meet me in battle, that thou mayest know me who I am, son of Deucalion, who was the son of Minos, who was the son of Zeus."

Then Deïphobus thought within himself, should he meet this man alone, or should he take some brave comrade with him? And it seemed to him better that he should take a brave comrade with him. Wherefore he went for Æneas, and found him in the rear of the battle, vexed at heart because King Priam did not honour him among the princes of Troy. Then said he—

"Come hither, Æneas, to fight for Alcathoüs, who was wont to care for thee when thou wast young, and now he lies dead under the spear of Idomeneus."

So they two went together; and Idomeneus saw them, but yielded not from his place, only called to his comrades that they should gather themselves together and help him. And on the other side Æneas called to Deïphobus, and Paris, and Agenor. So they fought about the body of Alcathoüs. Then did Æneas cast his spear at Idomeneus, but struck him not; but Idomeneus slew Œnomaüs, only when he would have spoiled him of his arms he could not, for the men of Troy pressed him hard, so that perforce he gave way. And as he turned, Deïphobus sought to slay him with his spear, but smote in his stead Ascalaphus, son of Ares. But when he would have spoiled him of his arms, Meriones struck him through the wrist with a spear. Straightway he dropped the helmet which he had seized, and Polites, his brother, led him out of the battle. And he climbed into his chariot and went back to the city. But the rest stayed not their hands from fighting, and many valiant heroes fell, both on this side and on that. For on the left the sons of Greece prevailed, so fiercely fought Idomeneus the Cretan, and Meriones, his comrade, and Antilochus, the son of Nestor, and Menelaüs; but on the right the Locrians and the Bœotians and the men of Athens could scarce keep Hector from the ships. Yet here for a while the battle went with them, for the Locrians, who were mighty archers, bent their bows against the men of Troy, and dismayed them, so thick flew the arrows, dealing wounds and death. Then said Polydamas to Hector—

"O Hector, thou art ever loath to hear counsel from others. Yet think not that because thou art stronger than other men, therefore Zeus hath also made thee wiser. For truly he gives diverse gifts to diverse men—strength to one and counsel to another. Hear, then, my words.

Thou seest that the Trojans keep not all together, for some stand aloof, while some fight, being few against many. Do thou therefore call the bravest together. Then shall we see whether we shall burn the ships, or, it may be, win our way back without harm to Troy; for indeed I forget not that there is a warrior here whom no man may match, nor will he, I trow, always keep aloof from the battle."

And the saying pleased Hector. So he went through the host looking for the chiefs—for Deïphobus, and Helenus, and Asius, and Acamas, son of Asius, and others, who were the bravest among the Trojans and allies. And some he found, and some he found not, for they had fallen in the battle, or had gone sorely wounded to the city. But at last he spied Paris, where he stood strengthening the hearts of his comrades.

"O Paris, fair of face, cheater of the hearts of women, where is Deïphobus, and Helenus, and Asius, and Acamas, son of Asius?"

But Paris answered him, "Some of these are dead, and some are sorely wounded. But we who are left fight on. Only do thou lead us against the Greeks, nor wilt thou say that we are slow to follow."

So Hector went along the front of the battle, leading the men of Troy. Nor did the Greeks give way when they saw him, but Ajax the Greater cried—

"Friend, come near, nor fear the men of Greece. Thou thinkest in thine heart to spoil the ships, but we have hands to keep them, and ere they perish Troy itself shall fall before us. Soon, I trow, wilt thou wish that thy horses were swifter than hawks, when they bear thee fleeing before us across the plain to the city."

But Hector answered, "Nay, thou braggart Ajax, what words are these? I would that I were as surely one of the Immortals as this day shall surely bring woe to the Greeks. And thou, if thou darest to meet my spear, shalt be slain among the rest, and feed with thy flesh the beasts of the field and the fowls of the air."

So he spake, and from this side and from that there went up a great cry of battle.

CHAPTER X.

THE BATTLE AT THE SHIPS (CONTINUED).

So loud was the cry, that it roused old Nestor where he sat in his tent, tending the wounded Machaon. Whereupon he said, "Sit thou here and drink the red wine till the fair Hecamedè shall have got ready the bath to wash the blood from thy wound, but I will ask how things fare in the battle."

So he went forth from the tent, seeking King Agamemnon. And lo! as he went the king met him, and with him were Diomed and Ulysses, who also had been wounded that day. So they held counsel together. And Agamemnon—for it troubled him sore that the people were slain—would that they should draw down the ships into the sea, and should flee homewards, as soon as the darkness should cover them and the Trojans should cease from the battle.

But Ulysses would have none of such counsel, saying, "Now surely, son of Atreus, thou art not worthy to rule over us, who have been men of war from our youth. Wilt thou leave this city, for the taking of which we have suffered so much? That may not be; let not any one of the Greeks hear the say such words. And what is this, that thou wouldst have us launch our ships now, whilst the hosts are fighting? Surely, so doing, we should perish altogether, for the Greeks would not fight any more, seeing that the ships were being launched, and the men of Troy would slay us altogether.

Then King Agamemnon said, "Thou speakest well." And he went through the host, bidding the men bear themselves bravely, and all the while Poseidon put courage and strength into their hearts. Then Hector cast his spear against Ajax Telamon. The shield kept it not off, for it passed beneath, but the two belts, of the shield and of the sword, stayed it, so that it wounded not his body. Then Hector in wrath and fear went back into the ranks of his comrades;

but as he went Ajax took a great stone—now were there many such which they had as props for the ships—and smote him above the rim of his shield, on the neck. As an oak falls, stricken by the thunder of Zeus, so he fell, and the Greeks rushed with a great cry to drag him to them, but could not, for all the bravest of the sons of Troy held their shields before him—Polydamas, and Æneas, and Sarpedon, and Glaucus. Then they carried him to the Xanthus, and poured water upon him. And after a while he sat up, and then again his spirit left him, for the blow had been very grievous. But when the Greeks saw that Hector had been carried out of the battle, they pressed on the more, slaying the men of Troy, and driving them back even out of the camp and across the trench. But when they came to their chariots, where they had left them on the other side of the trench, there they stood trembling and pale with fear. But Apollo, at the bidding of Zeus, went to Hector where he lay, and healed him of his wound, pouring strength and courage into his heart, so that he went back to the battle whole and sound. Then great fear came upon the Greeks when they saw him, and Thoas the Ætolian spake, saying—

"Surely this is a great marvel that I see with mine eyes. For we thought that Hector had been slain by the hand of Ajax, son of Telamon, and now, behold! he is come back to the battle. Many Greeks have fallen before him, and many, I trow, will fall, for of a truth some god has raised him up and helps him. But come, let all the bravest stand together. So, mighty though he be, he shall fear to enter our array."

And all the bravest gathered together and stood in the front, but the multitude made for the ships. But Hector came on, and Apollo before him, with his shoulders wrapped in cloud and the ægis shield in his hand. And many of the Greeks fell slain before the sons of Troy, as Iäsus of Athens, and Arcesilaüs the Bœotian, and Medon, who was brother to Ajax the Less, and many more. Thus the battle turned again, and came near to the trench; and now Apollo made it easy for the men of Troy to pass, so that they left not their chariots, as before, upon the brink, but drave them across.

Meanwhile Patroclus sat in the tent of Eurypylus, dressing his wound and talking with him. But when he saw what had chanced, he struck his thigh with his hand and cried—

"Now must I leave thee, Eurypylus, for I must haste to Achilles, so dreadful is now the battle. Perchance I may persuade him that he go forth to the fight."

So he ran to the tent of Achilles. And now the men of Troy were at the ships. And Hector and Ajax were fighting for one of them, and Ajax could not drive him back, and Hector could not burn the ship with fire. Then sprang forward Caletor with a torch in his hand, and Ajax smote him on the heart with a sword, so that he fell close by the ship. Then Hector cried—

"Come now, Trojans and allies, and fight for Caletor, that the Greeks spoil him not of his arms."

So saying he cast his spear at Ajax. Him he struck not, but Cytherius, his comrade, he slew. Then was Ajax sore dismayed, and spake to Teucer his brother—

"See now, Cytherius, our dear comrade, is dead, slain by Hector. But where are thy arrows and thy bow?"

So Teucer took his bow and laid an arrow on the string, and smote Clitus, who was charioteer to Polydamas. And then he aimed an arrow at Hector's self; but ere he could loose it, the bow-string was broken in his hands, and the arrow went far astray, for Zeus would not that Hector should so fall. Then Teucer cried aloud to his brother—

"Surely some god confounds our counsels, breaking my bow-string, which this very day I tied new upon my bow."

But Ajax said, " Let be thy bow, if it please not the gods, but take spear and shield and fight with the men of Troy. For though they master us to-day, they shall not take our ships for nought."

So Teucer armed himself afresh for the battle. But Hector, when he saw the broken bow, cried out—

"Come on, ye men of Troy, for Zeus is with us. Even now he broke the bow of Teucer, the great archer. And they whom Zeus helps prevail, and they whom he favours not grow weak. Come on ; for even though a man fall, it is well that he fall fighting for his fatherland ; .

and his wife and his children are safe, nor shall his glory cease, if so be that we drive the Greeks in their ships across the sea."

And on the other side Ajax, the son of Telamon, called to the Greeks, and bade them quit themselves like men. Then the battle grew yet fiercer, for Hector slew Schedius, who led the men of Phocis, and Ajax slew Laodamas, son of Antenor, and Polydamas Otus of Cyllene. Then Meges thought to slay Polydamas; but his spear went astray, smiting down Cræsmus; and Dolops, who was grandson to Laomedon, cast his spear at Meges, but the corslet stayed the point, though it pierced the shield. But Dolops' self Menelaüs smote through the shoulder, but could not spoil him of his arms, for Hector and his brothers hindered him. So they fought, slaying one another; but Hector still waxed greater and greater in the battle, and still the men of Troy came on, and still the Greeks gave way. So they came again, these pushing forward and these yielding ground, to the ships. And Hector caught hold of one of them, even the ship of Protesilaüs: him indeed it had brought from Troy, but it took him not back,

AJAX DEFENDING THE GREEK SHIPS AGAINST THE TROJANS.

for he had fallen, slain by the hand of Hector, as he leapt, first of all the Greeks, upon the shore of Troy. This Hector caught, and the battle raged like fire about it; for the men of Troy and the Greeks were gathered round, and none fought with arrows or javelins from afar, but man to man, with battle-axe and sword and great spears pointed at either end. And many a fair weapon lay shattered on the ground, and the earth flowed with blood as with a river. But still Hector held the stem of the ship with his hand, and called to the men of Troy that they should bring fire, for that Zeus had given them the victory that day. Then even Ajax himself gave way, so did the spears of the Trojans press him; for now he stood no longer upon the stern deck, but on the rowers' bench, thrusting thence with his spear at any one who sought to set fire to the ship. And ever he cried to the Greeks with a terrible voice—

"O ye Greeks, now must ye quit yourselves like men. For have ye any helpers behind? or have ye any walls to shelter you? No city is here, with well-built battlements, wherein ye might be safe, while the people should fight for you. For we are here in the plain of Troy, and the sea is close behind us, and we are far from our country. Wherefore all our hope is in valour, and not in shrinking back from the battle."

And still he thrust with his spear, if any of the men of Troy, at Hector's bidding, sought to bring fire against the ship. Full twelve he wounded where he stood.

CHAPTER XI.

THE DEEDS AND DEATH OF PATROCLUS.

And Patroclus stood by Achilles, weeping bitterly. Then said Achilles, "What ails thee, Patroclus, that thou weepest like a girl-child that runs along by her mother's side and would be taken up, holding her gown, and looking at her with tearful eyes till she lift her in her arms? Hast thou heard evil news from Phthia? Menœtius yet lives, they say, and Peleus. Or art thou weeping for the Greeks, because they perish for their folly?"

Then said Patroclus, "Be not wroth with me, great Achilles, for indeed the Greeks are in grievous straits, and all their bravest are wounded, and still thou cherishest thy wrath. Surely Peleus was not thy father, nor Thetis thy mother; but the rocks begat thee, and the sea brought thee forth. Or if thou goest not to the battle, fearing some warning from the gods, yet let me go, and thy Myrmidons with me. And let me put thy armour on me; so shall the Greeks have breathing space from the war."

So he spake, entreating, nor knew that for his own doom he entreated. And Achilles made reply—

"It is no warning that I heed, that I keep back from the war. But these men took from me my prize, which I won with my own hands. But let the past be past. I said that I would not rise up till the battle should come nigh to my own ships. But thou mayest put my armour upon thee, and lead my Myrmidons to the fight. For in truth the men of Troy are gathered as a dark cloud about the ships, and the Greeks have scarce standing-ground between them and the sea. For they see not the gleam of my helmet. And Diomed is not there with his spear; nor do I hear the voice of Agamemnon, but only the voice of Hector, as he calls the men of Troy to the battle. Go, therefore, Patroclus, and drive the fire from the ships. And then come thou back, nor fight any more with the Trojans, lest thou take my glory from me. And go not near, in the delight of battle, to the walls of Troy, lest one of the gods meet thee to thy hurt; and, of a truth, the keen archer Apollo loves them well."

But as they talked the one to the other, Ajax could hold out no longer. For swords and javelins came thick upon him, and clattered on his helmet, and his shoulder was weary with the great shield which he held; and he breathed heavily and hard, and the great drops of sweat fell upon the ground. Then at the last Hector came near and smote his spear with a great sword, so that the head fell off. Then was Ajax sore afraid, and gave way, and the men of Troy set torches to the ship's stem, and a great flame shot up to the sky. And Achilles saw it, and smote his thigh and spake—

"Haste thee, Patroclus, for I see the fire rising up from the ships. Put thou on the armour, and I will call my people to the war."

So Patroclus put on the armour—corslet and shield and helmet—and bound upon his shoulder the silver-studded sword, and took a mighty spear in his hand. But the great Pelian spear he took not, for that no man but Achilles might wield. Then Automedon yoked the horses to the chariot, Bayard and Piebald, and with them in the side harness, Pedasus; and they two were deathless steeds, but he was mortal.

Meanwhile Achilles had called the Myrmidons to battle. Fifty ships had he brought to Troy, and in each there were fifty men. Five leaders they had, and the bravest of the five was Pisander.

Then Achilles said, "Forget not, ye Myrmidons, the bold words that ye spake against the men of Troy during the days of my wrath, making complaint that I kept you from the battle against your will. Now, therefore, ye have that which you desired."

So the Myrmidons went to the battle in close array, helmet to helmet and shield to shield, close as the stones with which a builder builds a wall. And in front went Patroclus, and Automedon in the chariot beside him. Then Achilles went to his tent and took a great cup from the chest which Thetis his mother had given him. Now no man drank of that cup but he only, nor did he pour out of it libations to any of the gods but only to Zeus. This first he cleansed with sulphur, and then with water from the spring. And after this he washed his hands, and stood in the midst of the space before his tent, and poured out of it to Zeus, saying—

"O Zeus, I send my comrade to this battle; make him strong and bold, and give him glory, and bring him home safe to the ships, and my people with him."

So he prayed, and Father Zeus heard him, and part he granted and part denied.

But now Patroclus with the Myrmidons had come to where the battle was raging about the ship of Protesilaüs, and when the men of Troy beheld him, they thought that Achilles had forgotten his wrath, and was come forth to the war. And first Patroclus slew Pyræchmes, who was the chief of the Pæonians who live on the banks of the broad Axius. Then the men of Troy turned to flee, and many chiefs of fame fell by the spears of the Greeks. So the battle rolled back to the trench, and in the trench many chariots of the Trojans were broken, but the horses of Achilles went across it at a stride, so nimble were they and strong. And the heart of Patroclus was set to slay Hector; but he could not overtake him, so swift were his horses. Then did Patroclus turn his chariot, and keep back those that fled, that they should not go to the city, and rushed hither and thither, still slaying as he went.

But Sarpedon, when he saw the Lycians dismayed and scattered, called to them that they should be of good courage, saying that he would himself make trial of this great warrior. So he leapt down from his chariot, and Patroclus also leapt down, and they rushed at each other as two eagles rush together. Then first Patroclus struck down Thrasymelus, who was the comrade of Sarpedon; and Sarpedon, who had a spear in either hand, with the one struck the horse Pedasus, which was of mortal breed, on the right shoulder, and with the other missed his aim, sending it over the left shoulder of Patroclus. But Patroclus missed not his aim, driving his spear into Sarpedon's heart. Then fell the great Lycian chief, as an oak, or a poplar, or a pine falls upon the hills before the axe. But he called to Glaucus, his companion, saying—

"Now must thou show thyself a good warrior, Glaucus. First call the men of Lycia to fight for me, and do thou fight thyself, for it would be foul shame to thee, all thy days, if the Greeks should spoil me of my arms."

Then he died. But Glaucus was sore troubled, for he could not help him, so grievous was the wound where Teucer had wounded him. Therefore he prayed to Apollo, and Apollo helped him and made him whole. Then he went first to the Lycians, bidding them fight for their king, and then to the chiefs of the Trojans, that they should save the body of Sarpedon. And to Hector he said—

"Little carest thou for thy allies. Lo! Sarpedon is dead, slain by Patroclus. Suffer not the Myrmidons to carry him off and do dishonour to his body."

But Hector was troubled to hear such news, and so were all the sons of Troy, for Sarpedon was the bravest of the allies, and led most people to the battle. So with a great shout they charged and drove the Greeks back a space from the body; and then again the Greeks did the like. And so the battle raged, till no one would have known the great Sarpedon, so covered was he with spears and blood and dust. But at the last the Greeks drave back the men of Troy from the body, and stripped the arms, but the body itself they harmed not.

For Apollo came down at the bidding of Zeus and carried it out of the midst of the battle, and washed it with water, and anointed it with ambrosia, and wrapped it in garments of the gods. And then he gave it to Sleep and Death, and these two carried it to Lycia, his fatherland.

Then did Patroclus forget the word which Achilles had spoken to him, that he should not go near to Troy, for he pursued the men of the city even to the wall. Thrice he mounted on the angle of the wall, and thrice Apollo himself drove him back, pushing his shining shield. But the fourth time the god said, "Go thou back, Patroclus. It is not for thee to take the city of Troy; no, nor for Achilles, who is far better than thou art."

So Patroclus went back, fearing the wrath of the archer-god. Then Apollo stirred up the spirit of Hector, that he should go against Patroclus. Therefore he went, with his brother Cebriones for driver of his chariot. But when they came near, Patroclus cast a great stone which he had in his hand, and smote Cebriones on the forehead, crushing it in, so that he fell headlong from the chariot. And Patroclus mocked him, saying—

SLEEP AND DEATH CONVEYING THE BODY OF SARPEDON TO LYCIA.

"How nimble is this man! how lightly he dives! What spoil he would take of oysters, diving from a ship, even in a stormy sea! Who would have thought that there were such skilful divers in Troy!"

Then again the battle waxed hot about the body of Cebriones, and this too, at the last, the Greeks drew unto themselves, and spoiled it of the arms. And this being accomplished, Patroclus rushed against the men of Troy. Thrice he rushed, and each time he slew nine chiefs of fame. But the fourth time Apollo stood behind him and struck him on the head and shoulders, so that his eyes were darkened. And the helmet fell from off his head, so that the horsehair plumes were soiled with dust. Never before had it touched the ground, for it was the helmet of Achilles. And also the god brake the spear in his hand, and struck the shield from his arms, and loosed his corslet. All amazed he stood, and then Euphorbus, son of Panthoüs, smote him on the back with his spear, but slew him not. Then Patroclus sought to flee to the ranks of his comrades. But Hector saw him, and thrust at him with his spear, smiting him in the groin, so that he fell. And when the Greeks saw him fall, they sent up a terrible cry. Then Hector stood over him and cried—

"Didst thou think to spoil our city, Patroclus, and to carry away our wives and daughters in the ships? But, lo! I have slain thee, and the fowls of the air shall eat thy flesh; nor shall the great Achilles help thee at all—Achilles, who bade thee, I trow, strip the tunic from my breast, and thou thoughtest in thy folly to do it."

But Patroclus answered, "Thou boasteth much, Hector. Yet *thou* didst not slay me, but Apollo, who took from me my arms, for had twenty such as thou met me, I had slain them all. And mark thou this: death and fate are close to thee by the hand of the great Achilles."

And Hector answered, but Patroclus was dead already—

"Why dost thou prophesy death to me? May be the great Achilles himself shall fall by my hand."

Then he drew his spear from the wound, and went after Automedon, to slay him, but the swift horses of Achilles carried him away.

CHAPTER XII.

THE ROUSING OF ACHILLES.

FIERCE was the fight about the body of Patroclus, and many heroes fell, both on this side and on that, and first of them all Euphorbus, who, indeed, had wounded him. For as he came near to strip the dead man of his arms, Menelaüs slew him with his spear. He slew him, but took not his arms, for Hector came through the battle; nor did Menelaüs dare to abide his coming, but went back into the ranks of his own people. Then did Hector strip off the arms of Patroclus, the arms which the great Achilles had given him to wear. Then he laid hold of the body, and would have dragged it into the host of the Trojans, but Ajax Telamon came forth, and put his broad shield before it, as a lion stands before its cubs when the hunters meet it in the woods, drawing down over its eyes its shaggy brows. Then Hector gave place, but Glaucus saw him and said—

"Now is this a shame to thee, that thou darest not to stand against Ajax. How wilt thou and thy countrymen save the city of Troy? For surely no more will thy allies fight for it. Small profit have they of thee. Did not Sarpedon fall, and didst thou not leave him to be a prey to the dogs? And now, if thou hadst stood firm and carried off Patroclus, we might have made exchange, and gained from the Greeks Sarpedon and his arms. But it may not be, for thou fearest Ajax, and fleest before him."

But Hector said, "I fear him not, nor any man. Only Zeus gives victory now to one man and now to another. But wait thou here, and see whether I be a coward, as thou sayest."

Now he had sent the armour of Patroclus to the city. But now he ran after those that were carrying it, and overtook them, and put on the armour himself (but Zeus saw him doing it, and liked it not), and came back to the battle; and all who saw him thought that it had been the great Achilles himself. Then they all charged together, and fiercer grew the battle and fiercer as the day went on. For the Greeks said one to another, "Now had the earth better yawn and swallow us up alive, than we should let the men of Troy carry off Patroclus to their city;" and the Trojans said, "Now if we must all fall by the body of this man, be it so, but we will not yield." But the horses of Achilles stood apart from the battle, when they knew that Patroclus was dead, and wept. Nor could Automedon move them with the lash, nor with gentle words, nor with threats. They would not return to the ships, nor would they go into the battle; but as a pillar stands on the tomb of some dead man, so they stood, with their heads drooped to the ground, with the big tears dropping to the earth, and their long manes trailing in the dust.

But Father Zeus beheld them, and pitied them, and said—

"It was not well that we gave you, immortal as ye are, to a mortal man; for of all things that move on earth, mortal man is the fullest of sorrow. But Hector shall not possess you.

It is enough for him, yea, and too much, that he has the arms of Achilles."

Then did the horses move from their place and obey their charioteer as before. Nor could Hector take them, though he desired them very much. And all the while the battle raged about the dead Patroclus. And at last Ajax said to Menelaüs (now these two had borne themselves more bravely in the fight than all others)—

"See if thou canst find Antilochus, Nestor's son, that he may carry the tidings to Achilles, how that Patroclus is dead."

So Menelaüs went and found Antilochus on the left of the battle, and said to him, "I have ill news for thee. Thou seest, I trow, that the men of Troy have the victory to-day. And also Patroclus lies dead. Run, therefore, to Achilles, and tell him, if haply he may save the body; but as for the arms, Hector has them already."

Sore dismayed was Antilochus to hear such tidings, and his eyes were filled with tears and his voice was choked. Yet did he give heed to the words of Menelaüs, and ran to tell

Achilles of what had chanced. But Menelaüs went back to Ajax, where he had left him by Patroclus, and said—

"Antilochus, indeed, bears the tidings to Achilles. Yet I doubt whether he will come, for all his wrath against Hector, seeing that he has no armour to cover him. Let us think, then, how we may best carry Patroclus away from the men of Troy."

Then said Ajax, "Do thou and Meriones run forward and raise the body in your arms, and I and the son of Oileus will keep off meanwhile the men of Troy."

So Menelaüs and Meriones ran forward and lifted up the body. And the Trojans ran forward with a great shout when they saw them, as dogs run barking before the hunters when they chase a wild boar; but when the beast turns to bay, lo! they flee this way and that. So did the men of Troy flee when Ajax the Greater and Ajax the Less turned to give battle. But still the Greeks gave way, and still the Trojans came on, and ever in the front were Hector, the son of Priam, and Æneas, the son of Anchises. But in the mean time Antilochus came near to Achilles, who, indeed, seeing that the Greeks fled and the men of Troy pursued, was already sore afraid. And he said, weeping as he spake—

"I bring ill news—Patroclus lies low. The Greeks fight for his body, but Hector has his arms."

Then Achilles took of the dust of the plain in his hands, and poured it on his head, and lay at his length upon the ground, and tare his hair. And all the women wailed. And Antilochus sat weeping; but ever he held the hands of Achilles, lest he should slay himself in his great grief.

Then came his mother, hearing his cry, from where she sat in the depths of the sea, and laid her hand on him and said—

"Why weepest thou, my son? Hide not the matter from me, but tell me."

And Achilles answered, "All that Zeus promised thee for me he hath fulfilled. But what profit have I, for lo! my friend Patroclus is dead, and Hector has the arms which I gave him to wear. And as for me, I care not to live, except I can avenge me upon him."

Then said Thetis, "Nay, my son, speak not thus. For when Hector dieth, thy doom also is near."

And Achilles spake in great wrath: "Would that I might die this hour, seeing that I could not help my friend, but am a burden on the earth—I, who am better in battle than all the Greeks besides. Cursed be the wrath that sets men to strive the one with the other, even as it set me to strive with King Agamemnon! But let the past be past. And as for my fate—let it come when it may, so that I first avenge myself on Hector. Wherefore seek not to keep me back from the battle."

Then Thetis said, "Be it so; only thou canst not go without thy arms, which Hector hath. But to-morrow will I go to Hephæstus, that he may furnish thee anew."

But while they talked the men of Troy pressed the Greeks more and more, and the two heroes, Ajax the Greater and Ajax the Less, could no longer keep Hector back, but that he should lay hold of the body of Patroclus. And indeed he would have taken it, but that Zeus sent Iris to Achilles, who said—

"Rouse thee, son of Peleus, or Patroclus will be a prey for the dogs of Troy!"

But Achilles said, "How shall I go?—for arms have I none, nor know I whose I might wear. Haply I could shift with the shield of Ajax, son of Telamon, but he, I know, is carrying it in the front of the battle."

Then answered Iris, "Go only to the trench and show thyself; so shall the men of Troy tremble and cease from the battle, and the Greeks shall have breathing space."

So he went, and Athené put her ægis about his mighty shoulders, and a golden halo about his head, making it shine as a flame of fire, even as the watch-fires shine at night from some city that is besieged. Then went he to the trench; with the battle he mingled not, heeding his mother's commands, but he shouted aloud, and his voice was as the sound of a trumpet. And when the men of Troy heard, they were stricken with fear, and the horses backed with the chariots, and the drivers were astonished when they saw the flaming fire above his head which Athené had kindled. Thrice across the trench the great Achilles shouted, and thrice the men of Troy fell back. And that hour there perished twelve chiefs of fame, wounded by their own spears or trampled by their own steeds, so great was the terror among the men of Troy.

Right gladly did the Greeks take Patroclus out of the press. Then they laid him on a bier and carried him to the tent, Achilles walking with many tears by his side.

But on the other side the men of Troy held an assembly. Standing they held it, for none dared to sit, lest Achilles should be upon them.

Then spake Polydamas: "Let us not wait here for the morning. It was well for us to fight at the ships while Achilles yet kept his wrath against Agamemnon. But now it is not so. For to-morrow he will come against us in his anger, and many will fall before him. Wherefore let us go back to the city, for high are the walls and strong the gates, and he will perish before he pass them."

Then said Hector, "This is ill counsel, Polydamas. Shall we shut ourselves up in the city, where all our goods are wasted already, buying meat for the people? Nay, let us watch to-night, and to-morrow will we fight with the Greeks. And if Achilles be indeed come forth from his tent, be it so. I will not shun to meet him, for Ares gives the victory now to one man and now to another."

So he spake, and all the people applauded, foolish, not knowing what the morrow should bring forth.

CHAPTER XIII.

THE BATTLE AT THE RIVER.

MEANWHILE in the camp of the Greeks they mourned for Patroclus. And Achilles stood among his Myrmidons and said—

"Vain was the promise that I made to Menœtius that I would bring back his son with his portion of the spoils of Troy. But Zeus fulfils not the thoughts of man. For he lies dead, nor shall I return to the house of Peleus, my father, for I, too, must die in this land. But thee, O Patroclus, I will not bury till I bring hither the head and the arms of Hector, and twelve men of Troy to slay at thy funeral pile."

So they washed the body of Patroclus and anointed it, putting ointment into the wounds, and laid it on a bed, and covered it with a veil from the head to the feet.

Then went Thetis to the palace of Hephæstus, to pray him that he would make arms for her son. And the lady his wife, whose name was Grace, bade her welcome, and said—

"Why comest thou, Thetis? for thou art not wont to come hither, though thou art dear to us."

Then she called to her husband that Thetis sought him, and he answered from his forge where he wrought—

"Dear is Thetis to me, for she saved me in the old time, when my mother would have put me away because that I was lame. Greet her therefore for me; right willingly will I pay her what she deserves at my hands." Then he came from his forge and sat down by the goddess, and asked her, "What wantest thou?"

Then did Thetis tell him of her son Achilles, and of the wrong that had been done to him, and of his wrath, and of how Patroclus was dead, and the arms that he had had were lost.

Then said Hephæstus, "Be of good cheer: I will make what thou askest. Would that I could as easily keep from him the doom of death."

Then Hephæstus wrought at his forge. And first of all he made a mighty shield. On it he wrought the earth, and the sky, and the sea, and the sun, and the moon, and all the stars. He wrought also two cities. In the one there was peace, and about the other there was war. For in the first they led a bride to her home with music and dancing, and the women stood in the doors to see the show, and in the market-place the judges judged about one that had been slain, and one man said that he had paid the price of blood, and the other denied. But about the other city there sat an army besieging it, and the men of the city stood upon the wall, defending it. These had also set an ambush by a river where the herds were wont to drink. And when the herds came down, they rose up and took them, and slew the herdsmen. But the army of the besiegers heard the cry, and came swiftly on horses, and fought by the bank of the river. Also he wrought one field where many men drove the plough, and another where reapers reaped the corn, and boys gathered it in their arms to bind into sheaves, while the lord stood glad at heart beholding them. Also he wrought a vineyard, wherein was a path, and youths and maidens bearing baskets of grapes, and in the midst a boy played on a harp of gold and sang a pleasant song. Also he made a herd of oxen going from the stables to the pastures, and herdsmen and dogs, and in the front two lions had caught a mighty bull and were devouring it, while the dogs stood far off and barked. Also he made a sheepfold; also a marvellous dance of men and maidens, and these had coronets of gold, and those daggers of gold hanging from belts of silver. And round about the shield he wrought the great river of ocean. Besides the shield, he also made a corslet brighter than fire, and a great helmet with a crest of gold, and greaves of tin.

But all the while Achilles sat mourning for Patroclus, and his comrades wept about him. And at dawn Thetis brought him the arms and laid them before him. Loud they rattled on the ground, and all the Myrmidons trembled to hear; but when Achilles saw them his eyes blazed with fire, and he rejoiced in his heart. Only he said to his mother that he feared lest the body should decay, but she answered—

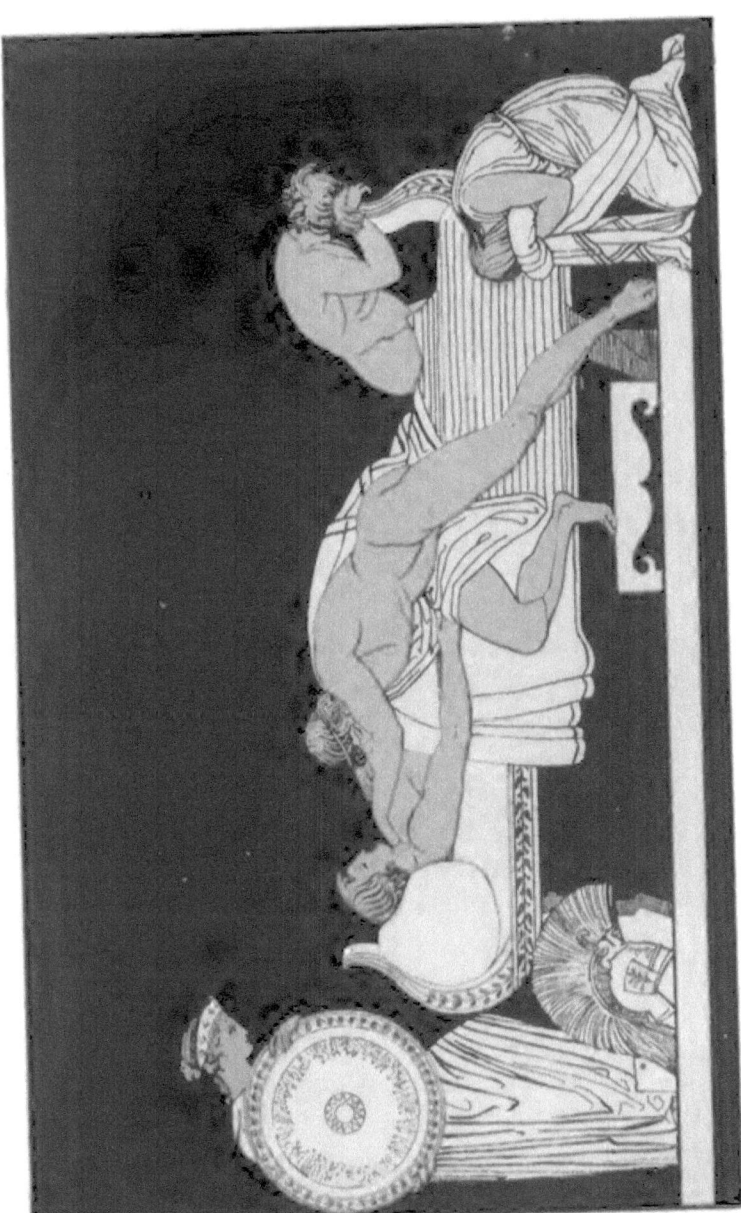

THETIS BRINGING THE ARMOUR TO ACHILLES.

"Be not troubled about this, for I will see to it. Make thy peace with Agamemnon, and go to the battle."

Then Achilles went along the shore and called the Greeks to an assembly, shouting mightily; and all, even those who were wont to abide in the ships, listened to his voice and came. So the assembly was gathered, and Achilles stood up in the midst, saying that he had put away his wrath; and King Agamemnon, sitting on his throne (for his wound hindered him from standing), said that he repented him of the wrong which he had done, only that Zeus had turned his thoughts to folly; but now he would give to Achilles all that Ulysses had promised on his behalf. And Achilles would have led the Greeks straightway to battle, but the wise Ulysses hindered him, saying that it was not well that he should send them to the fight fasting. Then did Agamemnon send to the tents of Achilles all the gifts that he had promised, and with them the maiden Briseïs. But she, when she came and saw Patroclus, beat her breast and her fair neck and face, and wailed aloud, for he had been gentle and good, she said. And all the women wailed with her, thinking each of her own sorrows.

Then the chiefs would have Achilles feast with them; but he hearkened not, for he would neither eat nor drink till he had had vengeance for the dead. And he spake, saying—

"Often, Patroclus, hast thou ordered the feast when we were hastening to the war. And now thou liest slain, and for grief for thee I cannot eat nor drink. For greater sorrow could not have come to me, not though Peleus himself were dead, or my young son Neoptolemus. Often did I think that I only should perish here, but that thou shouldest return and show him all that was mine—goods and servants and palace."

And as he wept the old men wept with him, thinking each of what he had left at home.

But after this the Greeks were gathered to the battle, and Achilles shone in the midst with the arms of Hephæstus upon him, and he flashed like fire. Then he spake to his horses—

"Take heed, Bayard and Piebald, that you save your driver to-day, nor leave him dead on the field, as you left Patroclus."

Then Heré gave to the horse Bayard a voice,

so that he spake: "Surely we will save thee, great Achilles; yet, for all that, doom is near to thee, nor are we the cause, but the gods and mastering Fate. Nor was it of us that Patroclus died, but Apollo slew him, and gave the glory to Hector. So shalt thou, too, die by the hands of a god and of a mortal man."

And Achilles said, "What need to tell me of my doom? Right well I know it. Yet will I not cease till I have made the Trojans weary of battle."

Then with a shout he rushed to the battle. And first there met him Æneas. Now Achilles cared not to fight with him, but bade him go back to his comrades. But Æneas would not, but told him of his race, how that he came from Zeus on his father's side, and how that his mother was Aphrodité, and that he held himself a match for any mortal man. Then he cast his spear, which struck the shield of Achilles with so dreadful a sound that the hero feared lest it should pierce it through, knowing not that the gifts of the gods are not easy for mortal man to vanquish. Two folds indeed it pierced that were of bronze, but in the gold it was stayed, and there were yet two of tin within. Then Achilles cast his spear. Through the shield of Æneas it passed, and though it wounded him not, yet was he sore dismayed, so near it came. Then Achilles drew his sword and rushed on Æneas, and Æneas caught up a great stone to cast at him. But it was not the will of the gods that Æneas should perish, seeing that he and his sons after him should rule over the men of Troy in the ages to come. Therefore Poseidon lifted him up and bore him over the ranks of men to the left of the battle, but first he drew the spear out of the shield and laid it at the feet of Achilles. Much the hero marvelled to see it, crying—

"This is a great wonder that I see with mine eyes. For, lo! the spear is before me, but the man whom I sought to slay I see not. Of a truth Æneas spake truth, saying that he was dear to the immortal gods."

Then he rushed into the battle, slaying as he went. And Hector would have met him, but Apollo stood by him and said, "Fight not with Achilles, lest he slay thee." Therefore he went back among the men of Troy. Many did

Achilles slay, and among them Polydorus, son of Priam, who, because he was the youngest and very dear, his father suffered not to go to the battle. Yet he went, in his folly, and being very swift of foot, he trusted in his speed, running through the foremost of the fighters. But as he ran Achilles smote him and wounded him to the death. But when Hector saw it he could not bear any more to stand apart. Therefore he rushed at Achilles, and Achilles rejoiced to see him, saying, " This is the man who slew my comrade." But they fought not then, for when Hector cast his spear Athené turned it aside, and when Achilles charged, Apollo bore Hector away.

Then Achilles turned to the others, and slew multitudes of them, so that they fled, part across the plain, and part to the river, the eddying Xanthus. And these leapt into the water as locusts leap into a river when the fire which men light drives them from the fields. And all the river was full of horses and men. Then Achilles leapt into the stream, leaving his spear on the bank, resting on the tamarisk trees. Only his sword had he, and with this he slew many; and they were as fishes which fly from some great dolphin in the sea. In all the bays of a harbour they hide themselves, for the great beast devours them apace. So did the Trojans hide themselves under the banks of the river. And when Achilles was weary of slaying he took twelve alive, whom he would slay on the tomb of Patroclus. Nor was there but one who dared to stand up against him, and this was Asteropæus, who was the grandson of the river god Axius, and led the men of Pæonia. And Achilles wondered to see him, and said—

"Who art thou, that standest against me?"

And he said, "I am the grandson of the river god Axius, fairest of all the streams on the earth, and I lead the men of Pæonia."

And as he spake he cast two spears, one with each hand, for he could use either alike; and the one struck the shield, nor pierced it through, for the gold stayed it, and the other grazed the right hand so that the blood spurted forth. Then did Achilles cast his spear, but missed his aim, and the great spear stood fast in the bank. And thrice Asteropæus strove to draw it forth. Thrice he strove in vain, and the fourth time he strove to break the spear. But as he strove Achilles smote him that he died. Yet had he some glory, for that he wounded the great Achilles.

But Priam stood on a tower of the wall and saw the people. Sore troubled was he, and he hastened down to the gates and said to the keepers, "Keep the wicket-gates in your hands open, that the people may enter in, for they fly before Achilles." So the keepers held the wicket-gates in their hands, and the people hastened in, wearied with toil and thirst, and covered with dust, and Achilles followed close upon them. And that hour would the Greeks have taken the city of Troy, but that Apollo saved it. For he put courage into the heart of Antenor's son Agenor, standing also by him, that he should not be slain. Therefore Agenor stood, thinking within himself—

"Shall I now flee with these others? Nay, for not the less will Achilles take me and slay me, and I shall die as a coward dies. Or shall I flee across the plain to Ida, and hide me in the thickets, and come back at nightfall to the city? Yet should he see me he will overtake me and smite me, so swift of foot is he and strong. But what if I stand to meet him before the gates? Well, he, too, is a mortal man, and his flesh may be pierced by the spear."

Therefore he stood till Achilles should come near. And when he came he cast his spear, striking the leg below the knee, but the greave turned off the spear, so strong was it. But when Achilles would have slain him, lo! Apollo lifted him up and set him within the city. And that the men of Troy might have space to enter, he took upon him Agenor's shape. And the false Agenor fled, and Achilles pursued. But meanwhile the men of Troy flocked into the city, nor did they stay to ask who was safe and who was dead, in such haste and fear did they flee.

CHAPTER XIV.

THE DEATH OF HECTOR.

THE Trojans were now safe in the city, refreshing themselves after all their grievous toil. Only Hector remained outside the walls, standing in front of the great Scæan gates. But all the while Achilles was fiercely pursuing the false Agenor, till at last Apollo turned and spake to him—

"Why dost thou pursue me, swift-footed Achilles? Hast thou not yet found out that I am a god, and that all thy fury is in vain? And now all the sons of Troy are safe in their city, and thou art here, far out of the way, seeking to slay me, who cannot die."

In great wrath Achilles answered him, " Thou hast done me wrong in so drawing me away from the wall, great archer, most mischief-loving of all the gods that are. Had it not been for this, many a Trojan more had bitten the ground. Thou hast robbed me of great glory, and saved thy favourites. O that I had the power to take vengeance on thee! Thou hadst paid dearly for thy cheat!"

Then he turned and rushed towards the city, swift as a racehorse whirls a chariot across the plain. Old Priam spied him from the walls, with his glittering armour, bright as that brightest of the stars—men call it Orion's dog—which shines at vintage-time, a baleful light, bringing the fevers of autumn to men. And the old man groaned aloud when he saw him, and stretching out his hands, cried to his son Hector, where he stood before the gates, eager to do battle with this dread warrior—

"Wait not for this man, dear son, wait not for him, lest thou die beneath his hand, for indeed he is stronger than thou. Wretch that he is! I would that the gods bare such love to him as I bear! Right soon would the dogs and vultures eat him. Of many brave sons has he bereaved me. Two I miss to-day—Polydorus and Lycaon. May be they are yet alive in the host of the Greeks, and I shall buy them back with gold, of which I have yet great store in my house. And if they are dead, sore grief will it be to me and to the mother who bare them; but little will care the other sons of Troy, so that thou fall not beneath the hand of Achilles Come within the walls, dear child; come to save the sons and daughters of Troy; come in pity for me, thy father, for whom, in my old age, an evil fate is in store, to see sons slain with the sword, and daughters carried into captivity, and babes dashed upon the ground. Ay, and last of all, the dogs which I have reared in my palace will devour me, lapping my blood and tearing my flesh as I lie on the threshold of my home. That a young man should fall in battle and suffer such lot as happens to the slain, this is to be borne; but that such dishonour should be done to the white hair and white beard of the old, mortal eyes can see no fouler sight than this."

Thus old Priam spake, but could not turn the heart of his son. And from the wall on the other side of the gate his mother called to him, weeping sore, and if perchance she might thus move his pity, she bared her bosom in his sight, and said—

"Pity me, my son; think of the breast which I gave thee in the old days, and stilled thy cries. Come within the walls; wait not for this man, nor stand in battle against him. If he slay thee, nor I, nor thy wife, shall pay thee the last honours of the dead, but far away by the ships of the Greeks the dogs and vultures will devour thee."

So father and mother besought their son, but all in vain. He was still minded to abide the coming of Achilles. Just as in the mountains a great snake at its hole abides the coming of a man: fierce glare its eyes, and it coils its tail about its hole: so Hector waited for Achilles; and as he waited he thought thus within himself—

"Woe is me if I go within the walls! Polydamas will be the first to reproach me, for he advised me to bring back the sons of Troy to the city before the night when Achilles roused himself to war. But I would not listen to him. Would that I had! it had been much better for us; but now I have destroyed the people by my folly. I fear the sons and daughters of Troy, what they may say; I fear lest some coward reproach me: 'Hector trusted in his strength, and lo! he has destroyed the people.' Better were it for me either to slay Achilles or to fall by his hand with honour here before the walls. Or, stay: shall I put down my shield, and lay aside my helmet, and lean my spear against the wall and go to meet the great Achilles, and promise that we will give back the fair Helen, and all the wealth that Paris carried off with her; ay, and render up all the wealth that there is in the city, that the Greeks may divide it among themselves, binding the sons of Troy with an oath that they keep nothing back? But this is idle talk: he will have no shame or pity, but will slay me while I stand without arms or armour before him. It is not for us to talk as a youth and a maiden talk together. It is better to meet in arms, and see whether the ruler of Olympus will give victory to him or to me."

Thus he thought in his heart; and Achilles came near, brandishing over his right shoulder the great Pelian spear, and the flash of his arms was as the flame of fire, or as the rising sun. And Hector trembled when he saw him, nor dared to abide his coming. Fast he fled from the gates, and fast Achilles pursued him, as a hawk, fastest of all the birds of air, pursues a dove upon the mountains. Past the watch-tower they ran, past the wind-blown fig-tree, along the waggon-road which went about the walls, and they came to the fair-flowing fountain where from two springs rises the stream of eddying Scamander. Hot is one spring, and a steam ever goes up from it, as from a burning fire; and cold is the other, cold, even in the summer heats, as hail or snow or ice. There are fair basins of stone, where the wives and fair daughters of Troy were wont to wash their garments, but that was in the old days of peace, or ever the Greeks came to the land. Past the springs they ran, one flying, the other pursuing: brave was he that fled, braver he that pursued; it was no sheep for sacrifice or shield of ox-hide for which they ran, but for the life of Hector, the tamer of horses. Thrice they ran round the city, and all the gods looked on.

And Zeus said, "This is a piteous sight that I behold. My heart is grieved for Hector—Hector, who has ever worshipped me with sacrifice, now on the heights of Ida, and now in the citadel of Troy; and now the great Achilles is pursuing him round the city of Priam. Come, ye gods, let us take counsel together. Shall we save him from death, or let him fall beneath the hand of Achilles?"

Then Athené said, "What is this that thou sayest, great sire?—to rescue a man whom fate has appointed to die? Do it, if it be thy will; but we, the other gods, approve it not."

Zeus answered her, "My heart is loath; yet I would do thee pleasure. Be it as thou wilt."

Then Athené came down in haste from the top of Olympus, and still Hector fled and Achilles pursued, just as a dog pursues a fawn upon the hills. And ever Hector made for the gates, or to get shelter beneath the towers, if haply those that stood upon them might defend him with their spears; and ever Achilles would get before him, and drive him towards the plain. So they ran, one making for the city, and the other driving him to the plain. Just as in a dream, when one seems to fly and another seems to pursue, and the one cannot escape and the other cannot overtake, so these two ran together. But as for Hector, Apollo even yet helped him, and gave him strength and nimble knees, else could he not have held out against Achilles, who was swiftest of foot among the sons of men.

Now Achilles had beckoned to the Greeks that no man should throw his spear at Hector, lest, perchance, he should be robbed of his glory. And when the two came in their running for the fourth time to the springs of Scamander, Zeus held out the great balance of doom, and in one scale he put the fate of Achilles, and in the other the fate of Hector; and lo! the scale of Hector sank down to the realms of death, and Apollo left him.

Then Athené lighted down from the air close to Achilles and said, "This, great Achilles, is our day of glory, for we shall slay Hector, mighty warrior though he be. For it is his doom to die, and not Apollo's self shall save him. But stand thou still and take breath, and I will give this man heart to meet thee in battle."

So Achilles stood, leaning upon his spear. And Athené took the shape of Deïphobus, and came near to Hector and said—

"Achilles presses thee hard, my brother, pursuing thee thus round the city of Priam. Come, let us make a stand and encounter him."

Then Hector answered him, "Deïphobus, I always loved thee best of all my brothers; but now I love thee yet more, for that thou alone, while all others remained within, hast ventured forth to stand by my side."

But the false Deïphobus said, "Much did father and mother and all my comrades beseech me to remain. But my heart was sore troubled for thee, and I could not stay. But let us stand and fight this man, not stinting our spears, and see whether he shall carry our spoil to the ships or we shall slay him here."

Then the two chiefs came near to each other, and Hector with the waving plume spake first and said, "Thrice, great Achilles, hast thou pursued me round the walls of Troy, and I dared not stand up against thee; but now I fear thee no more. Only let us make this covenant between us: if Zeus give me the victory, I will do no dishonour to thy body; thy arms and armour will I take, and give back thy body to the Greeks; and do thou promise to do likewise."

But Achilles scowled at him and said, "Hector, talk not of covenants to me. Men and lions make no oaths between each other, neither is there any agreement between wolves and sheep. So there shall be no covenant between me and thee. One of us two shall fall; and now is the time for thee to show thyself a warrior, for of a truth Athené will slay thee by my spear, and thou shalt pay the penalty for all my comrades whom thou hast slain."

Then he threw the mighty spear, but Hector saw it coming and avoided it, crouching on the ground, so that the mighty spear flew above his head and fixed itself in the earth. But Athené snatched it from the ground and gave it back to Achilles, Hector not perceiving.

Then Hector spake to Achilles: "Thou hast missed thy aim, great Achilles. It was no word of Zeus that thou spakest, prophesying my doom, but thou soughtest to cheat me, terrifying me by thy words. Thou shalt not drive thy steel into my back, but here into my breast, if the gods will it so. But now look out for my spear. Would it might bury itself in thy flesh. The battle would be easier for the men of Troy were thou only out of the way."

And as he spake he threw his long-shafted spear. True aim he took, for the spear struck the very middle of Achilles' shield. It struck, but pierced it not, but bounded far away, for the shield was not of mortal make. And Hector stood dismayed, for he had not another spear, and when he called to Deïphobus that he should give him another, lo! Deïphobus was gone. Then Hector knew that his end was come, and he said to himself, " Now have the gods called me to my doom. I thought that Deïphobus was near ; but he is within the walls, and the help which he promised me was but a cheat with which Athené cheated me. Zeus and Apollo are with me no more ; but, if I must die, let me at least die in such a deed as men of after time may hear of."

So he spake, and drew the mighty sword that hung by his side : then, as an eagle rushes through the clouds to pounce on a leveret or a lamb, rushed on the great Achilles. But he dealt never a blow ; for Achilles charged to meet him, his shield before his breast, his helmet bent forward as he ran, with the long plumes streaming behind, and the gleam of his spear-point was as the gleam of the evening star, which is the fairest of all the stars in heaven. One moment he thought where he should drive it home, for the armour which Hector had won from Patroclus guarded him well; but one spot there was, where by the collar-bone the neck joins the shoulder (and nowhere is the stroke of sword or spear more deadly). There he drave in the spear, and the point stood out behind the neck, and Hector fell in the dust.

Then Achilles cried aloud, "Hector, thou thoughtest in the day when thou didst spoil Patroclus of his arms that thou wouldst be safe from vengeance, taking, forsooth, no account of me. And lo! thou art fallen before me, and now the dogs and vultures shall devour thee, but to him all the Greeks shall give due burial."

But Hector, growing faint, spake to him. "Nay, great Achilles, by thy life, and by thy knees, and by thy parents dear, I pray thee, let not the dogs of the Greeks devour me. Take rather the ransom, gold and bronze, that my father and mother shall pay thee, and let the sons and daughters of Troy give me burial rites."

But Achilles scowled at him, and cried, " Dog, seek not to entreat me! I could mince that flesh of thine and devour it raw, such grief hast thou wrought me. Surely the dogs shall devour thee, nor shall any man hinder. No ransom, though it were ten times told, should buy thee back; no, not though Priam should offer thy weight in gold."

Then Hector, who was now at the point to die, spake to him. " I know thee well, what manner of man thou art, that the heart in thy breast is iron only. Only beware lest some vengeance from the gods come upon thee in the day when Paris and Apollo shall slay thee, for all thy valour, by the Scæan gates."

So speaking, he died. But Achilles said, "Die, hound; but my fate I meet when Zeus and the other gods decree."

Then he drew his spear out of the corpse and stripped off the arms; and all the Greeks came about the dead man, marvelling at his stature and beauty, and no man came but wounded the dead corpse. And one would say to another, "Surely this Hector is less dreadful now than in the day when he would burn our ships with fire."

Then Achilles devised a ruthless thing in his heart. He pierced the ankle-bones of Hector, and so bound the body with thongs of ox-hide to the chariot, letting the head drag behind, the head that once was so fair, and now was so disfigured in the dust. So he dragged Hector to the ships. And Priam saw him from the walls, and scarce could his sons keep him back, but that he should go forth and beg the body of his dear son from him who had slain him. And Hecuba his mother also bewailed him, but Andromaché knew not as yet of what had befallen. For she sat in her dwelling, wearing a great purple mantle broidered with flowers. And she bade her maidens make ready a bath for Hector, when he should come back from the battle, nor knew that he should never need it more. But the voice of wailing from the town came to her, and she rose up hastily in great fear, and dropped the shuttle from her hand and called to her maidens—

ANDROMACHE FAINTING ON THE WALL.

"Come with me, ye maidens, that I may see what has befallen, for I heard the voice of Queen Hecuba, and I fear me much that some evil has come to the children of Priam. For it may be that Achilles has run between Hector and the city, and is pursuing him to the plain, for never will Hector abide with the army, but will fight in the front, so bold is he."

Then she hasted through the city like as she were mad. And when she came to the wall she stood and looked; and lo! the horses of Achilles were dragging Hector to the ships. Then did darkness come on her, and she fell back fainting, and from her fair head dropped the net and the wreath and the diadem which golden Aphrodité gave her on the day when Hector of the waving plume took her from the house of Eëtion to be his wife.

CHAPTER XV.

THE RANSOMING OF HECTOR.

AND after a while, at the bidding of Zeus, Thetis went to Achilles and found him weeping softly for his dead friend, for the strength of his sorrow was now spent, and she said to him, "It is the will of the gods that thou give up the body of Hector, and take in exchange the ransom of gold and precious things which his father will give thee for him."

And her son answered, "Be it so, if the gods will have it."

Then Zeus sent Iris, who was his messenger, to King Priam, where he sat with his face wrapped in his mantle, and his sons weeping about him, and his daughters wailing through the chambers of his palace.

Then Iris spake. "Be of good cheer, Priam, son of Dardanus; Zeus has sent me to thee.

Go, taking with thee such gifts as may best please the heart of Achilles, and bring back the body of thy dear son Hector. Go without fear of death or harm, and go alone. Only let an aged herald be with thee, to help thee when thou bringest back the body of the dead."

Then Priam rose with joy, and bade his sons bring forth his chariot; but first he went to his chamber, and called to Hecuba, his wife, and told her of his purpose, nor heeded when she sought to turn him from it, but said, " Seek not to hold me back, nor be a bird of evil omen in my house. If any prophet or seer had bidden me do this thing, I should have held it a deceit; but now have I heard the very voice of the messenger of Zeus. Wherefore, I shall go. And if I die, what care I? Let Achilles slay me, so that I embrace once more the body of my son."

Then he bade put into a waggon shawls and mantles that had never been washed, and rugs and cloaks and tunics, twelve of each, and ten talents of gold, and two bright three-footed caldrons, and four basins, and a cup of passing beauty which the Thracians had given him.

The old man spared nothing that he had, if only he might buy back his son. None of the Trojans would he suffer to come near him. "Begone," he cried, "ye cowards! Have ye nothing to wail for at home, that ye come to wail with me? Surely, an easy prey will ye be to the Greeks, now that Hector is dead."

Then he cried with like angry words to his sons, Paris, and Agathon, and Deïphobus, and the others—there were nine of them in all—

"Make haste, ye evil brood. Would that ye all had died in the room of Hector. Surely an ill-fated father am I. Many a brave son I had, as Mestor, and Troilus, and Hector, who was fairer than any of the sons of men. But all these are gone, and only the cowards are left, masters of lying words, and skilful in the dance, and mighty to drink wine. But go, yoke the mules to the waggon."

So they yoked the mules to the waggon. But the horses for his chariot Priam, with the herald, yoked himself.

Then Hecuba came near, and bade a woman-servant come and pour water on his hands.

And when she had poured, King Priam took a great cup from the hands of his wife, and made a libation to Zeus, and prayed—

"Hear me, Father Zeus, and grant that Achilles may pity me. And do thou send me now a lucky sign, that I may go with a good heart to the ships of the Greeks."

And Zeus heard him, and sent an eagle, a mighty bird, whose wings spread out on either side as wide as is the door of some spacious chamber in a rich man's house. On his right hand it flew high above the city, and all rejoiced when they saw the sign.

Then the old man mounted his chariot in haste, and drove forth from the palace. Before him the mules drew the four-wheeled waggon, and these the herald Idæus guided. But his chariot the old king drove himself. And all his kinsfolk went with him, weeping as for one who was going to his death. But when they came down from the city to the plain, Priam and the herald went towards the ships of the Greeks, but all the others returned to Troy.

But Zeus saw him depart, and said to Hermes, "Hermes, go, guide King Priam to the ships of the Greeks, so that no man see him before he comes to the tents of Achilles."

Then Hermes fastened on his feet the fair sandals of gold with which he flies, fast as the wind, over sea and land, and in his hand he took the rod with which he opens and closes, as he wills, the eyes of men. And he flew down and lighted on the plain of Troy, taking on him the likeness of a fair youth.

But when they had driven past the great tomb of Ilus, they stopped the horses and the mules, to let them drink of the river. And darkness came over the land; and then the herald spied Hermes, and said—

"Consider, my lord, what we shall do. I see a man, and I am sore afraid lest he slay us. Shall we flee on the chariot, or shall we go near and entreat him, that he may have pity upon us?"

Then the old man was sore troubled, and his hair stood up with fear. But Hermes came near and took him by the hand and said—

"Whither goest thou, old man, with thy horses and mules through the darkness? Hast thou no fear of these fierce Greeks, who are close at hand? If any one should see thee with all this wealth, what then? And thou art not young, nor is thy attendant young, that ye should defend yourselves against an enemy. But I will not harm thee, nor suffer any other, for thou art like my own dear father."

"It is well, my son," said the old man. "Surely one of the blessed gods is with me, in causing me to meet such an one as thou, so fair and so wise. Happy the parents of such a son!"

And Hermes said, "Come, tell me true, old man. Are you sending away all these treasures that they may be kept safe for you far away? or are all the men of Troy leaving the city, seeing now that Hector, who was their bravest warrior, is dead?"

Then Priam answered, "Who art thou, my son, and what thy race, that thou speakest so truly about my hapless son?"

"Often," said Hermes, "have I seen Hector in the battle, both at other times, and when he drove the Greeks before him at the ships. We, indeed, stood and watched and marvelled at him, for Achilles would not suffer us to fight, being wroth with King Agamemnon. Now, I am a follower of Achilles, coming from Greece in the same ship with him. One of the Myrmidons I am, son of Polyctor, an old man such as thou art. Six other sons he has, and when we drew lots who should come to the war, it fell to me. But know that with the morning the Greeks will set their battle in array against the city, for they are weary of their sojourn, and the kings cannot keep them back."

Then said Priam, "If thou art an attendant of Achilles, tell me true, is my son yet by the ships, or have the dogs devoured him?"

And Hermes answered, "Nor dogs nor vultures have devoured him. Still he lies by the ships of Achilles; and though this is the twelfth day since he was slain, no decay has touched him. Nay, though Achilles drags him round the tomb of his dear Patroclus, yet even so does no unseemliness come to him. All fresh he lies, and the blood is washed from him, and all his wounds are closed—and many spear-points pierced him. The blessed gods love him well, dead man though he be."

This King Priam was well pleased to hear. "It is well," he said, "for a man to honour the gods; for, indeed, as my son never forgot the dwellers on Olympus, so have they not forgotten him, even in death. But do thou take this fair cup, and do kindness to him, and lead me to the tent of Achilles."

"Nay," answered Hermes; "thou speakest this in vain. No gift would I take from thy hand unknown to Achilles; for I honour him much, and fear to rob him, lest some evil happen to me afterwards. But thee I will guide to Argos itself, if thou wilt, whether by land or sea, and no one shall blame my guiding."

Then he leapt into the chariot of the king and caught the reins in his hand, and gave the horses and the mules a strength that was not their own. And when they came to the ditch and the trench that guarded the ships, lo! the guards were busy with their meal; but Hermes, made sleep descend upon them, and opened the gates, and brought in Priam with his treasures. And when they came to the tent of Achilles, Hermes lighted down from the chariot and said—

"Lo! I am Hermes, whom my father, Zeus, hath sent to be thy guide. And now I shall depart, for I would not that Achilles should see me. But go thou in, and clasp his knees, and beseech him by his father and his mother and his child. So shalt thou move his heart with pity."

So Hermes departed to Olympus, and King Priam leapt down from the chariot, leaving the herald to care for the horses and the mules, and went to the tent. There he found Achilles sitting; his comrades sat apart, but two waited on him, for he had but newly ended his meal, and the table was yet at his hand. But no man saw King Priam till he was close to Achilles, and caught his knees and kissed his hands, the dreadful, murderous hands that had slain so many of his sons. As a man who slays another by mishap flies to some stranger land, to some rich man's home, and all wonder to see him, so Achilles wondered to see King Priam, and his comrades wondered, looking one at another. Then King Priam spake—

"Think of thy father, godlike Achilles, and pity me. He is old, as I am, and, it may be, his neighbours trouble him, seeing that he has no defender; yet so long as he knows that thou art alive, it is well with him, for every day he hopes to see his dear son returned from Troy. But as for me, I am altogether wretched. Many a valiant son I had—nineteen born to me of one mother—and most of them are dead, and he that was the best of all, who kept our city safe, he has been slain by thee. He it is whom I have come to ransom. Have pity on him and on me, thinking of thy father. Never, surely, was lot so sad as this, to kiss the hands that slew a son."

But the words so stirred the heart of Achilles that he wept, thinking now of Patroclus, and now of his old father at home; and Priam wept, thinking of his dead Hector. But at last Achilles stood up from his seat and raised King Priam, having pity on his white hair and his white beard, and spake—

"How didst thou dare to come to the ships of the Greeks, to the man who slew thy sons? Surely thou must have a heart of iron. But sit thou down: let our sorrows rest in our hearts, for there is no profit in lamentation. It is the will of the gods that men should suffer woe, but they are themselves free from care. Two chests are set by the side of Father Zeus, one of good and one of evil gifts, and he mixes the lot of men, taking out of both. Many noble gifts did the gods give to King Peleus: wealth and bliss beyond that of other men, and kingship over the Myrmidons. Ay! and they gave him a goddess to be his wife. But they gave also this evil, that he had no stock of stalwart children in his house, but one son only, and I cannot help him at all in his old age, for I tarry here far away in Troy. Thou, too, old man, hadst wealth and power of old, and lordship over all that lies between Lesbos and Phrygia and the stream of Hellespont. And to thee the gods have given this ill, that there is ever battle and slaughter about thy city walls. But as for thy son, wail not for him, for thou canst not raise him up."

But Priam answered, "Make me not to sit, great Achilles, while Hector lies unhonoured. Let me ransom him, and look upon him with my eyes, and do thou take the gifts. And the gods grant thee to return safe to thy fatherland."

But Achilles frowned and said, "Vex me

not; I am minded myself to give thee back thy Hector. For my mother came from the sea, bearing the bidding of Zeus, and thou, methinks, hast not come hither without some guidance from the gods. But trouble me no more, lest I do thee some hurt."

And King Priam feared and held his peace. Then Achilles hastened from his tent, and two comrades with him. First they loosed the horses from the chariot and the mules from the waggon; then they brought in the herald Idæus, and took the gifts. Only they left of them two cloaks and a tunic, wherein they might wrap the dead. And Achilles bade the women wash and anoint the body, but apart from the tent, lest, perchance, Priam should see his son and cry aloud, and so awaken the fury in his heart. But when it was washed and anointed, Achilles himself lifted it in his arms and put it on the litter, and his comrades lifted the litter on the waggon.

And when all was finished, Achilles groaned and cried to his dead friend, saying—

"Be not wroth, Patroclus, if thou shouldst hear in the unknown land that I have ransomed Hector to his father: a noble ransom hath he paid me, and of this, too, thou shalt have thy share, as is meet."

Then he went back to his tent, and set himself down over against Priam, and spake: "Thy son is ransomed, old man, and to-morrow shalt thou see him and take him back to Troy. But now let us eat. Did not Niobe eat when she lost her twelve children, six daughters and six blooming sons, whom Apollo and Artemis slew — Apollo these and Artemis those — because she likened herself to the fair Latona? So let us eat, old man. To-morrow shalt thou weep for Hector; many tears, I trow, shall be shed for him."

So they ate and drank. And when the meal was ended, Achilles sat and marvelled at King Priam's noble look, and King Priam marvelled at Achilles, so strong he was and fair.

Then Priam said, "Let me sleep, great Achilles. I have not slept since my son fell by thy hand. Now I have eaten and drunk, and my eyes are heavy."

So the comrades of Achilles made him a bed outside, where no one might see him, should it chance that any of the chiefs should come to the tent of Achilles to take counsel, and should espy him, and tell it to King Agamemnon.

But before he slept King Priam said, "If thou art minded to let me bury Hector, let there be a truce between my people and the Greeks. For nine days let us mourn for Hector, and on the tenth will we bury him and feast the people, and on the eleventh raise a great tomb above him, and on the twelfth we will fight again, if fight we must."

And Achilles answered, "Be it so: I will stay the war for so long."

But while Priam slept there came to him Hermes, the messenger of Zeus, and said: "Sleepest thou, Priam, among thy foes? Achilles has taken ransom for thy Hector; but thy sons that are left would pay thrice as much for thee should Agamemnon hear that thou wert among the ships."

The old man heard and trembled, and roused the herald, and the two yoked the horses and the mules. So they passed through the army, and no man knew. And when they came to the river, Hermes departed to Olympus, and the morning shone over all the earth. Wailing and weeping, they carried the body to the city.

It was Cassandra who first espied them as they came. Her father she saw, and the herald, and then the dead body on the litter, and she cried, "Sons and daughters of Troy, go to meet Hector, if ever ye have met him with joy as he came back from the battle."

And straightway there was not man or woman left in the city. They met the waggon when it was close to the gates: his wife led the way, and his mother and all the multitude followed. And in truth they would have kept it thus till evening, weeping and wailing, but King Priam spake—

"Let us pass; ye shall have enough of wailing when we have taken him to his home."

So they took him to his home and laid him on his bed. And the minstrels lamented, and the women wailed.

Then first of all came Andromaché, his wife, and cried—

"O my husband, thou hast perished in thy youth, and I am left in widowhood, and our child, thy child and mine, is but an infant! I fear me he will not grow to manhood. Ere that day this city will fall, for thou art gone who wast its defender. Soon will they carry us away, mothers and children, in the ships, and thou, my son, perchance wilt be with us, and serve the stranger in unseemly bondage; or, it may be, some Greek will slay thee, seizing thee and dashing thee from the wall: some Greek whose brother, or father, or son, Hector has slain in the battle. Many a Greek did Hector slay; no gentle hand was his in the fray. Therefore do the people wail for him to-day. Sore is thy parents' grief, O Hector, but sorest mine. Thou didst stretch no hands of farewell to me from thy bed, nor speak any word of comfort for me to muse on while I weep night and day."

Next spake Hecuba, his mother. "Dear wast thou, my son, in life to the immortal gods, and dear in death. Achilles dragged thee about the tomb of his dear Patroclus, but could not bring him back, I ween, and now thou liest fresh and fair as one whom the god of the silver bow has slain with sudden stroke."

And last of all came Helen, and cried, "Many

a year has passed since I came to Troy—would that I had died before! And never have I heard from thy lips one bitter word, and if ever husband's sister, or sister-in-law, or mother-in-law—for Priam was ever gentle as a father—spake harshly to me, thou wouldst check them with thy grace and gracious words. Therefore I weep for thee; no one is left to be my friend in all the broad streets of Troy. All shun and hate me now."

And all the people wailed reply.

Then Priam spake. "Go, my people, gather wood for the burial, and fear not any ambush of the Greeks, for Achilles promised that he would stay the war until the twelfth day should come."

So for nine days the people gathered much wood, and on the tenth they laid Hector upon the pile, and lit fire beneath it. And when it was burnt they quenched the embers with wine. Then his brethren and comrades gathered together the white bones, and laid them in a chest of gold; and this they covered with purple robes and put in a great coffin, and laid upon it stones many and great. And over all they raised a mighty mound; and all the while the watchers watched, lest the Greeks should arise and slay them. Last of all was a great feast held in the palace of King Priam.

So they buried Hector, the tamer of horses.

THE ODYSSEY;

OR,

THE ADVENTURES OF ULYSSES.

CHAPTER I.

THE CYCLOPS.

When the great city of Troy was taken, all the chiefs who had fought against it set sail for their homes. But there was wrath in heaven against them, for indeed they had borne themselves haughtily and cruelly in the day of their victory. Therefore they did not all find a safe and happy return. For one was shipwrecked, and another was shamefully slain by his false wife in his palace, and others found all things at home troubled and changed, and were driven to seek new dwellings elsewhere. And some, whose wives and friends and people had been still true to them through those ten long years of absence, were driven far and wide about the world before they saw their native land again. And of all, the wise Ulysses was he who wandered farthest and suffered most.

He was well-nigh the last to sail, for he had tarried many days to do pleasure to Agamemnon, lord of all the Greeks. Twelve ships he had with him—twelve he had brought to Troy—and in each there were some fifty men, being scarce half of those that had sailed in them in the old days, so many valiant heroes slept the last sleep by Simoïs and Scamander, and in the plain and on the sea-shore, slain in battle or by the shafts of Apollo.

First they sailed north-west to the Thracian coast, where the Ciconians dwelt, who had helped the men of Troy. Their city they took, and in it much plunder, slaves and oxen, and jars of fragrant wine, and might have escaped unhurt, but that they stayed to hold revel on the shore. For the Ciconians gathered their neighbours, being men of the same blood, and did battle with the invaders, and drove them to their ship. And when Ulysses numbered his men, he found that he had lost six out of each ship.

Scarce had he set out again when the wind began to blow fiercely; so, seeing a smooth sandy beach, they drave the ships ashore and dragged them out of reach of the waves, and waited till the storm should abate. And the third morning being fair, they sailed again, and journeyed prosperously till they came to the very end of the great Peloponnesian land, where Cape Malea looks out upon the southern sea. But contrary currents baffled them, so that they could not round it, and the north wind blew so strongly that they must fain drive before it. And on the tenth day they came to the land where the lotus grows—a wondrous fruit, of which whosoever eats cares not to see country or wife or children again. Now the Lotus-eaters, for so they called the people of the land, were a kindly folk, and gave of the fruit to some of the sailors, not meaning them any harm, but thinking it to be the best that they had to give. These, when they had eaten, said that they would not sail any more over the sea ; which, when the wise Ulysses heard, he bade their comrades bind them and carry them, sadly complaining, to the ships.

Then, the wind having abated, they took to their oars, and rowed for many days till they came to the country where the Cyclopes dwell. Now, a mile or so from the shore there was an island, very fair and fertile, but no man dwells there or tills the soil, and in the island a harbour where a ship may be safe from all winds, and at the head of the harbour a stream falling from a rock, and whispering alders all about it. Into this the ships passed safely, and were hauled up on the beach, and the crews slept by them, waiting for the morning. And the next day they hunted the wild goats, of which there was great store on the island, and feasted right merrily on what they caught, with draughts of red wine which they had carried off from the town of the Ciconians.

But on the morrow, Ulysses, for he was ever fond of adventure, and would know of every land to which he came what manner of men they were that dwelt there, took one of his twelve ships and bade row to the land. There was a great hill sloping to the shore, and there rose up here and there a smoke from the caves where the Cyclopes dwelt apart, holding no converse with each other, for they were a rude and savage folk, but ruled each his own household, not caring for others. Now very close to the shore was one of these caves, very huge and deep, with laurels round about the mouth, and in front a fold with walls built of rough stone, and shaded by tall oaks and pines. So Ulysses chose out of the crew the twelve bravest, and bade the rest guard the ship, and went to see what manner of dwelling this was, and who abode there. He had his sword by his side, and on his shoulder a mighty skin of wine, sweet-smelling and strong, with which he might win the heart of some fierce savage, should he chance to meet with such, as indeed his prudent heart forecasted that he might.

So they entered the cave, and judged that it was the dwelling of some rich and skilful shepherd. For within there were pens for the young of the sheep and of the goats, divided all according to their age, and there were baskets full of cheeses, and full milkpails ranged along the wall. But the Cyclops himself was away in the pastures. Then the companions of Ulysses besought him that he would depart, taking with him, if he would, a store of cheeses and sundry of the lambs and of the kids. But he would not, for he wished to see, after his wont, what manner of host this strange shepherd might be. And truly he saw it to his cost!

It was evening when the Cyclops came home, a mighty giant, twenty feet in height, or more. On his shoulder he bore a vast bundle of pine logs for his fire, and threw them down outside the cave with a great crash, and drove the flocks within, and closed the entrance with a huge rock, which twenty waggons and more could not bear. Then he milked the ewes and all the she-goats, and half of the milk he curdled for cheese, and half he set ready for himself, when he should sup. Next he kindled a fire with the pine logs, and the flame lighted up all the cave, showing him Ulysses and his comrades.

"Who are ye?" cried Polyphemus, for that was the giant's name. "Are ye traders, or, haply, pirates?"

For in those days it was not counted shame to be called a pirate.

Ulysses shuddered at the dreadful voice and shape, but bore him bravely, and answered, "We are no pirates, mighty sir, but Greeks, sailing back from Troy, and subjects of the great King Agamemnon, whose fame is spread from one end of heaven to the other. And we are come to beg hospitality of thee in the name of Zeus, who rewards or punishes hosts and guests according as they be faithful the one to the other, or no."

"Nay," said the giant, "it is but idle talk to tell me of Zeus and the other gods. We Cyclopes take no account of gods, holding ourselves to be much better and stronger than they. But come, tell me where have you left your ship?"

But Ulysses saw his thought when he asked about the ship, how he was minded to break it, and take from them all hope of flight. Therefore he answered him craftily—

"Ship have we none, for that which was ours King Poseidon brake, driving it on a jutting rock on this coast, and we whom thou seest are all that are escaped from the waves."

Polyphemus answered nothing, but without more ado caught up two of the men, as a man might catch up the whelps of a dog, and dashed them on the ground, and tore them limb from limb, and devoured them, with huge draughts of milk between, leaving not a morsel, not even the very bones. But the others, when they saw the dreadful deed, could only weep and pray to Zeus for help. And when the giant had ended his foul meal, he lay down among his sheep and slept.

Then Ulysses questioned much in his heart whether he should slay the monster as he slept, for he doubted not that his good sword would pierce to the giant's heart, mighty as he was. But, being very wise, he remembered that, should he slay him, he and his comrades would yet perish miserably. For who should move away the great rock that lay against the door of the cave? So they waited till the morning. And the monster woke, and milked his flocks, and afterwards, seizing two men, devoured them for his meal. Then he went to the pastures, but put the great rock on the mouth of the cave, just as a man puts down the lid upon his quiver.

All that day the wise Ulysses was thinking what he might best do to save himself and his companions, and the end of his thinking was this: there was a mighty pole in the cave, green wood of an olive tree, big as a ship's mast, which Polyphemus purposed to use, when the smoke should have dried it, as a walking staff. Of this he cut off a fathom's length, and his comrades sharpened it and hardened it in the fire, and then hid it away. At evening the giant came back, and drove his sheep into the cave, nor left the rams outside, as he had been wont to do before, but shut them in. And having duly done his shepherd's work, he made his cruel feast as before. Then Ulysses came forward with the wine-skin in his hand, and said—

"Drink, Cyclops, now that thou hast feasted. Drink, and see what precious things we had in our ship. But no one hereafter will come to thee with such like, if thou dealest with strangers as cruelly as thou hast dealt with us."

Then the Cyclops drank, and was mightily pleased, and said, "Give me again to drink, and tell me thy name, stranger, and I will give thee a gift such as a host should give. In good truth this is a rare liquor. We, too, have vines, but they bear not wine like this, which indeed must be such as the gods drink in heaven."

Then Ulysses gave him the cup again, and he drank. Thrice he gave it to him, and thrice he drank, not knowing what it was, and how it would work within his brain.

Then Ulysses spake to him. "Thou didst ask my name, Cyclops. Lo! my name is No Man. And now that thou knowest my name, thou shouldst give me thy gift."

And he said, "My gift shall be that I will eat thee last of all thy company."

And as he spoke he fell back in a drunken sleep. Then Ulysses bade his comrades be of good courage, for the time was come when they should be delivered. And they thrust the stake of olive wood into the fire till it was ready, green as it was, to burst into flame, and they thrust it into the monster's eye; for he had but one eye, and that in the midst of his forehead, with the eyebrow below it. And Ulysses leant with all his force upon the stake, and thrust it in with might and main. And the burning wood hissed in the eye, just as the red-hot iron hisses in the water when a man seeks to temper steel for a sword.

Then the giant leapt up, and tore away the

ULYSSES GIVING WINE TO POLYPHEMUS.

stake, and cried aloud, so that all the Cyclopes who dwelt on the mountain side heard him and came about his cave, asking him, "What aileth thee, Polyphemus, that thou makest this uproar in the peaceful night, driving away sleep? Is any one robbing thee of thy sheep, or seeking to slay thee by craft or force?"

And the giant answered, "No Man slays me by craft."

"Nay, but," they said, "if no man does thee wrong, we cannot help thee. The sickness which great Zeus may send, who can avoid? Pray to our father, Poseidon, for help."

Then they departed; and Ulysses was glad at heart for the good success of his device, when he said that he was No Man.

But the Cyclops rolled away the great stone from the door of the cave, and sat in the midst, stretching out his hands, to feel whether perchance the men within the cave would seek to go out among the sheep.

Long did Ulysses think how he and his comrades should best escape. At last he lighted upon a good device, and much he thanked Zeus for that this once the giant had driven the rams with the other sheep into the cave. For, these being great and strong, he fastened his comrades under the bellies of the beasts, tying them with osier twigs, of which the giant made his bed. One ram he took, and fastened a man beneath it, and two others he set, one on either side. So he did with the six, for but six were left out of the twelve who had ventured with him from the ship. And there was one mighty ram, far larger than all the others, and to this Ulysses clung, grasping the fleece tight with both his hands. So they waited for the morning. And when the morning came, the rams rushed forth to the pasture; but the giant sat in the door and felt the back of each as it went by, nor thought to try what might be underneath. Last of all went the great ram. And the Cyclops knew him as he passed, and said—

" How is this, thou, who art the leader of the flock? Thou art not wont thus to lag behind. Thou hast always been the first to run to the pastures and streams in the morning, and the first to come back to the fold when evening fell; and now thou art last of all. Perhaps thou art troubled about thy master's eye, which some wretch—No Man, they call him—has destroyed, having first mastered me with wine. He has not escaped, I ween. I would that thou couldst speak, and tell me where he is lurking. Of a truth I would dash out his brains upon the ground, and avenge me of this No Man."

So speaking, he let him pass out of the cave. But when they were out of reach of the giant, Ulysses loosed his hold of the ram, and then unbound his comrades. And they hastened to their ship, not forgetting to drive before them a good store of the Cyclops' fat sheep. Right glad were those that had abode by the ship to see them. Nor did they lament for those that had died, though they were fain to do so, for Ulysses forbade, fearing lest the noise of their weeping should betray them to the giant, where they were. Then they all climbed into the ship, and sitting well in order on the benches, smote the sea with their oars, laying-to right lustily, that they might the sooner get away from the accursed land. And when they had rowed a hundred yards or so, so that a man's voice could yet be heard by one who stood upon the shore, Ulysses stood up in the ship and shouted—

"He was no coward, O Cyclops, whose comrades thou didst so foully slay in thy den. Justly art thou punished, monster, that devourest thy guests in thy dwelling. May the gods make thee suffer yet worse things than these!"

Then the Cyclops, in his wrath, broke off the top of a great hill, a mighty rock, and hurled it where he had heard the voice. Right in front of the ship's bow it fell, and a great wave rose as it sank, and washed the ship back to the shore. But Ulysses seized a long pole with both hands and pushed the ship from the land, and bade his comrades ply their oars, nodding with his head, for he was too wise to speak, lest the Cyclops should know where they were. Then they rowed with all their might and main.

And when they had gotten twice as far as before, Ulysses made as if he would speak again; but his comrades sought to hinder him, saying, "Nay, my lord, anger not the giant any more. Surely we thought before we were lost, when he threw the great rock, and washed our ship back to the shore. And if he hear thee now, he may crush our ship and us, for the man throws a mighty bolt, and throws it far."

But Ulysses would not be persuaded, but stood up and said, "Hear, Cyclops! If any man ask who blinded thee, say that it was the warrior Ulysses, son of Laertes, dwelling in Ithaca."

And the Cyclops answered with a groan, "Of a truth, the old oracles are fulfilled, for long ago there came to this land one Telemus, a prophet, and dwelt among us even to old age. This man foretold to me that one Ulysses would rob me of my sight. But I looked for a great man and a strong, who should subdue me by force, and now a weakling has done the deed, having cheated me with wine. But come thou hither, Ulysses, and I will be a host indeed to thee. Or, at least, may Poseidon give thee such a voyage to thy home as I would wish thee to have. For know that Poseidon is my sire. May be that he may heal me of my grievous wound."

And Ulysses said, "Would to God I could send thee down to the abode of the dead, where thou wouldst be past all healing, even from Poseidon's self."

Then Cyclops lifted up his hands to Poseidon and prayed—

"Hear me, Poseidon, if I am indeed thy son and thou my father. May this Ulysses never reach his home! or, if the Fates have ordered that he should reach it, may he come alone, all his comrades lost, and come to find sore trouble in his house!"

And as he ended he hurled another mighty rock, which almost lighted on the rudder's end, yet missed it as by a hair's breadth. So Ulysses and his comrades escaped, and came to the island of the wild goats, where they found their comrades, who indeed had waited long for them, in sore fear lest they had perished. Then Ulysses divided amongst his company all the sheep which they had taken from the Cyclops. And all, with one consent, gave him for his share the great ram which had carried him out of the cave, and he sacrificed it to Zeus. And all that day they feasted right merrily on the flesh of sheep and on sweet wine, and when the night was come, they lay down upon the shore and slept.

CHAPTER II.

THE ISLAND OF ÆOLUS—THE LÆSTRYGONS—CIRCÉ.

AFTER sailing awhile, they came to the island of Æolus, who is the king of the winds, and who dwelt there with his children, six sons and six daughters. Right well did Æolus entertain them, feasting them royally for a whole month, while he heard from Ulysses the story of all that had been done at Troy. And when Ulysses prayed him that he would help him on his way homewards, Æolus hearkened to him, and gave him the skin of an ox in which he had bound all contrary winds, so that they should not hinder him. But he let a gentle west wind blow, that it might carry him and his comrades to their home. For nine days it blew and now they were near to Ithaca, their country, so that they saw lights burning in it, it being night-time. But now, by an ill chance, Ulysses fell asleep, being wholly wearied out, for he had held the helm for nine days, nor trusted it to any of his comrades. And while he slept his comrades, who had cast eyes of envy on the great ox-hide, said one to another—

"Strange it is how men love and honour this Ulysses whithersoever he goes. And now he comes back from Troy with much spoil, but we with empty hands. Let us see what it is that Æolus hath given, for doubtless in this ox-hide is much silver and gold."

So they loosed the great bag of ox-hide, and lo! all the winds rushed out, and carried them far away from their country. But Ulysses, waking with the tumult, doubted much whether he should not throw himself into the sea and so die. But he endured, thinking it better to live. Only he veiled his face and so sat, while the ships drave before the winds, till they came once more to the island of Æolus. Then Ulysses went to the palace of the king, and found him feasting with his wife and children, and sat him down on the threshold. Much did they wonder to see him, saying, "What evil power has hindered thee, that thou didst not reach thy country and home?"

Then he answered, "Blame not me, but the evil counsels of my comrades, and sleep, which mastered me to my hurt. But do ye help me again."

But they said, "Begone: we may not help him whom the gods hate; and hated of them thou surely art."

So Æolus sent him away. Then again they launched their ships and set forth, toiling wearily at the oars, and sad at heart.

Six days they rowed, nor rested at night, and on the seventh they came to Lamos, which was a city of the Læstrygons, in whose land the night is as the day, so that a man might earn double wage, if only he wanted not sleep —shepherd by day and herdsman by night. There was a fair haven with cliffs about it, and a narrow mouth with great rocks on either side. And within are no waves, but always calm.

Now Ulysses made fast his ship to the rocks, but the others entered the haven. Then he sent two men and a herald with them, and these came upon a smooth road by which waggons brought down wood from the mountain to the city. Here they met a maiden, the stalwart daughter of Antiphates, king of the land, and asked of her who was lord of that country. Whereupon she showed them her father's lofty palace. And they, entering this, saw the maiden's mother, big as a mountain, horrible to behold, who straightway called to Antiphates, her husband. The messengers, indeed, fled to the ships; but he made a great shout, and the Læstrygons came flocking about him, giants, not men. And these broke off great stones from the cliffs, each stone as much as a man could carry, and cast them at the ships, so that they were broken. And the men they speared, as if they were fishes, and devoured them. So it happened to all the ships in the haven. Ulysses only escaped, for he cut the hawser with his sword, and bade his men ply their oars, which indeed they did right willingly.

After a while they came to the island of Æœa, where Circé dwelt, who was the daughter of the Sun. Two days and nights they lay upon the shore in great trouble and sorrow. On the third, Ulysses took his spear and sword and climbed a hill that there was, for he wished to see to what manner of land they had come. And having climbed it, he saw the smoke rising from the palace of Circé, where it stood in the midst of a wood. Then he thought awhile: should he go straightway to the palace that he saw, or first return to his comrades on the shore? And this last seemed better; and it chanced that as he went he saw a great stag which was going down to the river to drink, for indeed the sun was now hot, and casting his spear at it he pierced it through. Then he fastened together the feet with green withes and a fathom's length of rope, and slinging the beast round his neck, so carried it to the ship, leaning on his spear; for indeed it was heavy to bear, nor could any man have carried it on the shoulder with one hand. And when he was come to the ship, he cast down his burden. Now the men were sitting with their faces muffled, so sad were they. But when he bade them be of good cheer, they looked up and marvelled at the great stag. And all that day they feasted on deer's flesh and sweet wine, and at night lay down to sleep on the shore. But when morning was come, Ulysses called them all together and spake—

"I know not, friends, where we are. Only I know, having seen smoke yesterday from the hill, that there is a dwelling in this island."

It troubled the men much to hear this, for they thought of the Cyclops and of the Læstrygons; and they wailed aloud, but there was no counsel in them. Wherefore Ulysses divided them into two companies, setting Eurylochus over the one and himself over the other, and shook lots in a helmet who should go and search out the island, and the lot of Eurylochus leapt out. So he went, and comrades twenty and two with him. And in an open space in the wood they found the palace of Circé. All about were wolves and lions; yet these harmed not the men, but stood up on their hind legs, fawning upon them, as dogs fawn upon their master when he comes from his meal. And the men were afraid. And they stood in the porch and heard the voice of Circé as she sang with a lovely voice and plied the loom. Then said Polites, who was dearest of all his comrades to Ulysses—

"Some one within plies a great loom, and sings with a loud voice. Some goddess is she, or woman. Let us make haste and call."

So they called to her, and she came out and beckoned to them that they should follow. So they went, in their folly. And she bade them sit, and mixed for them a mess, red wine, and in it barley-meal and cheese and honey, and mighty drugs withal, of which, if a man drank, he forgot all that he loved. And when they had drunk she smote them with her wand. And lo! they had of a sudden the heads and the voices and the bristles of swine, but the heart of a man was in them still. And Circé shut them in sties, and gave them mast and acorns and cornel to eat.

But Eurylochus fled back to the ship. And for a while he could not speak, so full was his heart of grief, but at the last he told the tale of what had befallen. Then Ulysses took his silver-studded sword and his bow, and bade Eurylochus guide him by the way that he had gone.

Nor would he hearken when Eurylochus would have hindered him, but said, "Stay here by the ship, eating and drinking, if it be thy will, but I must go, for necessity constrains me."

And when he had come to the house, there met him Hermes of the golden wand, in the shape of a fair youth, who said to him—

"Art thou come to rescue thy comrades that are now swine in Circé's house? Nay, but thou shalt never go back thyself. Yet, stay; I will give thee such a drug as shall give thee power to resist all her charms. For when she shall have mixed thee a mess, and smitten thee with her wand, then do thou rush upon her with thy sword, making as if thou wouldst slay her. And when she shall pray for peace, do thou make her swear by the great oath that binds the gods that she will not harm thee."

Then Hermes showed Ulysses a certain herb, whose root was black, but the flower white as milk. "Moly," the gods call it, and very hard it is for mortal man to find. Then Ulysses went into the house, and all befell as Hermes had told him. For Circé would have changed him as she had changed his comrades. Then he rushed at her with his sword, and made her

ULYSSES AT THE TABLE OF CIRCE.

swear the great oath which binds the gods that she would not harm him.

But afterwards, when they sat at meat together, the goddess perceived that he was silent and ate not. Wherefore she said, "Why dost thou sit, Ulysses, as though thou wert dumb? Fearest thou any craft of mine? Nay, but that may not be, for have I not sworn the great oath that binds the gods?"

And Ulysses said, "Nay, but who could think of meat and drink when such things had befallen his companions?"

Then Circé led the way, holding her wand in her hand, and opened the doors of the sties, and drove out the swine that had been men. Then she rubbed on each another mighty drug, and the bristles fell from their bodies and they became men, only younger and fairer than before. And when they saw Ulysses they clung to him and wept for joy, and Circé herself was moved with pity.

Then said she, "Go, Ulysses, to thy ship, and put away all the goods and tackling in the caves that are on the shore, but come again hither thyself, and bring thy comrades with thee."

Then Ulysses went. Right glad were they who had stayed to see him, glad as are the calves who have been penned in the fold-yard when their mothers come back in the evening. And when he told them what had been, and would have them follow him, they were all willing, save only Eurylochus, who said—

"O ye fools, whither are we going? To the dwelling of Circé, who will change us all into swine, or wolves, or lions, and keep us in prison, even as the Cyclops did! For was it not this same foolhardy Ulysses that lost our comrades there?"

Then was Ulysses very wroth, and would have slain Eurylochus, though near of kin to him. But his comrades hindered him, saying, "Let him abide here and keep the ship, if he will. But we will go with thee to the dwelling of Circé."

Then Ulysses forbore. Nor did Eurylochus stay behind, but followed with the rest. So they went to the dwelling of Circé, who feasted them royally, so that they remained with her for a whole year, well content.

But when the year was out they said to

Ulysses, "It were well to remember thy country, if it is indeed the will of the gods that thou shouldst return thither."

Then Ulysses besought Circé that she would send him on his way homewards, as indeed she had promised to do. And she answered—

"I would not have you abide in my house unwillingly. Yet must thou first go another journey, even to the dwellings of the dead, there to speak with the seer Tiresias."

But Ulysses was sore troubled to hear such things, and wept aloud, saying, "Who shall guide us in this journey?—for never yet did ship make such a voyage as this."

Then said Circé, "Seek no guide; only raise the mast of thy ship and spread the white sails, and sit in peace. So shall the north wind bear thee to the place on the ocean shore where are the groves of Persephoné, tall poplars and willows. There must thou beach thy ship. And after that thou must go alone."

Then she told him all that he must do if he would hold converse with the dead seer Tiresias, and hear what should befall him. So the next morning he roused his companions, telling them that they should now return. But it chanced that one of them, Elpenor by name, was sleeping on the roof, for the coolness, being heavy with wine. And when he heard the stir of his comrades, he rose up, nor thought of the ladder, but fell from the roof and brake his neck. And the rest being assembled, Ulysses told them how they must take another journey first, even to the dwellings of the dead. This they were much troubled to hear, yet they made ready the ship and departed.

CHAPTER III.

THE REGIONS OF THE DEAD—SCYLLA—THE OXEN OF THE SUN—CALYPSO.

So they came to the place of which Circé had told them. And when all things had been rightly done, Ulysses saw spirits of the dead. First of all came Elpenor, and he marvelled much to see him, saying—

"How camest thou hither?—on foot, or in the ship?"

Then he answered, telling how he had died, and he said, "Now, as thou wilt go back, I know, to the island of Circé, suffer me not to remain unburied, but make above me a mound of earth, for men in aftertimes to see, and put upon it my oar, with which I was wont to row while I yet lived."

These things Ulysses promised that he would do. Afterwards came the spirit of Tiresias, holding a sceptre of gold in his hand. And when Ulysses asked him of his return, he said—

"Thy return shall be difficult, because of the anger of Poseidon, whose son thou madest blind. Yet, when thou comest to the island of the Three Capes, where feed the oxen of the Sun, if thou leave these unhurt, thou and thy comrades shall return to Ithaca. But otherwise they shall perish, and thou shalt return, after long time, in a ship not thine own, and shalt find in thy palace, devouring thy goods, men of violence, suitors of thy wife. These shalt thou slay, openly or by craft. Nor yet shalt thou rest, but shalt go to a land where men know not the sea, nor eat their meat with salt; and thou shalt carry thy oar on thy shoulder. And this shall be a sign to thee, when another wayfarer, meeting thee, shall ask whether it be a winnowing fan that thou bearest on thy shoulder; then shalt thou fix thy oar in the earth, and make a sacrifice to Poseidon, and so return. So shalt thou die at last in peace."

Then Tiresias departed. After this he saw his mother, and asked how it fared with his home in Ithaca, and she told him all. And many others he saw, wives and daughters of the heroes of old time. Also there came King Agamemnon, who told him how Ægisthus, with Clytemnestra, his wicked wife, had slain him in his own palace, being newly returned from Troy. Fain would the king have heard how it fared with Orestes, his son, but of this Ulysses could tell him nothing. Then came the spirit of Achilles, and him Ulysses comforted, telling him how bravely and wisely his son Neoptolemus had borne himself in Troy.

Also he saw the spirit of Ajax, son of Telamon; but Ajax spake not to him, having great wrath in his heart, because of the arms of Achilles. For the two, Ajax and Ulysses, had contended for them, Achilles being dead, before the assembly of the Greeks, and the Greeks had given them to Ulysses, whereupon Ajax, being very wroth, had laid hands upon himself.

And having seen many other things, Ulysses went back to his ship, and returned with his companions to the island of Circé. And being arrived there, first they buried Elpenor, making a mound over him, and setting up on it his oar, and afterwards Circé made them a feast. But while the others slept she told to Ulysses all that should befall him, saying—

"First thou wilt come to the island of the Sirens, who sing so sweetly, that whosoever hears them straightway forgets wife and child and home. In a meadow they sit, singing sweetly, but about them are bones of men. Do thou, then, close with wax the ears of thy companions, and make them bind thee to the mast, so that thou mayest hear the song and yet take no hurt. And do thou bid them, when thou shalt pray to be loosed, not to hearken, but rather to bind thee the more. And this peril being past, there lie others in thy path, of which thou must take thy choice. For either thou must pass between the rocks which the gods call the Wanderers—and these close upon all that passes between them, even the very doves in their flight, nor has any ship escaped them, save only the ship Argo, which Heré loved — or thou must go through the strait, where there is a rock on either hand. In the one rock dwells Scylla, in a cave so high above the sea that an archer could not reach it with his arrow. A horrible monster is she.

Twelve unshapely feet she hath, and six long necks, and on each a head with three rows of teeth. In the cave she lies, but her heads are without, fishing for sea-dogs and dolphins, or even a great whale, if such should chance to go by. Think not to escape her, Ulysses, for, of a truth, with each head will she take one of thy companions. But the other rock is lower and more flat, with a wild fig-tree on the top. There Charybdis thrice a day draws in the dark water, and thrice a day sends it forth. Be not thou near when she draws it in; not even Poseidon's self could save thee. Choose rather to pass near to Scylla, for it is better to lose six of thy companions than that all should perish."

Then said Ulysses, "Can I not fight with this Scylla, and so save my companions?"

But Circé answered, "Nay, for she is not of mortal race. And if thou linger to arm thyself, thou wilt but lose six others of thy companions. Pass them with all the speed that may be, and call on Crataïs, who is the mother of Scylla, that she may keep her from coming the second time. Then wilt thou come to the island of the Three Capes, where feed the oxen of the Sun. Beware that thy companions harm them not."

The next day they departed. Then Ulysses told his companions of the Sirens, and how they should deal with him. And after a while, the following wind that had blown ceased, and there was a great calm; so they took down the sails and laid them in the ship, and put forth the oars to row. Then Ulysses made great cakes of wax, kneading them (for the sun was now hot), and put into the ears of his companions. And they bound him to the mast and so rowed on. Then the Sirens sang—

> "*Hither, Ulysses, great Achaian name,*
> *Turn thy swift keel, and listen to our lay;*
> *Since never pilgrim near these regions came,*
> *In black ship on the azure fields astray,*
> *But heard our sweet voice ere he sailed away,*
> *And in his joy passed on with ampler mind.*
> *We know what labours were in ancient day*
> *Wrought in wide Troia, as the gods assigned;*
> *We know from land to land all toils of all mankind.*" *

Then Ulysses prayed that they would loose him, nodding his head, for their ears were stopped; but they plied their oars, and Eurylochus and Perimedes put new bonds upon him.

* Worsley.

After this they saw a smoke and surf, and heard a mighty roar, and their oars dropped out of their hands for fear; but Ulysses bade them be of good heart, for that by his counsel they had escaped other dangers in past time. And the rowers he bade row as hard as they might. But to the helmsman he said, "Steer the ship outside the smoke and the surf, and steer close to the cliffs, lest the ship shoot off unawares and lose us." But of Scylla he said nothing, fearing lest they should lose heart and cease rowing altogether. Then he armed himself, and stood in the prow waiting till Scylla should appear.

But on the other side Charybdis was sucking in the water with a horrible noise, and with eddies so deep that a man might see the sand at the bottom. But while they looked trembling at this, Scylla caught six of the men from the ship, and Ulysses heard them call him by his name as the monster carried them away. And never, he said in after days, did he see with his eyes so piteous a sight.

But after this they came to the land where fed the oxen of the Sun. And Ulysses said, "Let us pass by this island, for there shall we find the greatest evil that we have yet suffered." But they would not hearken; only they said that the next day they would sail again.

Then spake Ulysses, "Ye constrain me, being many to one. Yet promise me this, that ye will not take any of the sheep or oxen, for if ye do great trouble will come to us."

So they promised. But for a whole month the south wind blew and ceased not. And their store of meat and drink being spent, they caught fishes and birds, as they could, being sore pinched with hunger. And at the last it chanced that Ulysses, being weary, fell asleep. And while he slept, his companions, Eurylochus persuading them, took of the oxen of the Sun, and slew them, for they said that their need was great, and that when they came to their own land they would build a temple to the Sun to make amends. But the Sun was very wroth with them. And a great and dreadful thing happened, for the hides crept, and the meat on the spits bellowed.

Six days they feasted on the oxen, and on the seventh they set sail. But when they were now out of sight of land, Zeus brought up a great storm over the sea, and a mighty west wind blew, breaking both the forestay and the backstay of the mast, so that it fell. And after this a thunderbolt struck the ship, and all the men that were in it fell overboard and died. But Ulysses lashed the keel to the mast with the backstay, and on these he sat, borne by the winds across the sea.

All night was he borne along, and in the morning he came to Charybdis. And it chanced that Charybdis was then sucking in the water; but Ulysses, springing up, clung to a wild fig-tree that grew from the rock, but could find no rest for his feet, nor yet could climb into the tree. All day long he clung, waiting till the raft should come forth again; and at evening, at the time when a judge rises from his seat after judging many causes, the raft came forth. Then he loosed his hands and fell, so that he sat astride upon the raft.

After this he was borne for nine days upon the sea, till he came to the island Ogygia, where dwelt the goddess Calypso.

CHAPTER IV.

TELEMACHUS AND PENELOPÉ.

In this island of Ogygia Ulysses abode seven years, much against his will, thinking always of his home and his wife and his young son. And when the seven years were ended, Athené, who had ever loved him much, spake to Zeus, complaining much that one so wise had been so long balked of his return.

Then said Zeus that it should not be so any longer, for that Poseidon must give up his wrath against the man, if all the other gods were of one mind.

Then said Athené to Zeus, " Do thou send Hermes, thy messenger, to Calypso, that she let Ulysses depart, and I will go to Ithaca to Telemachus, to bid him go search for his father; for indeed it is but seemly that he should do so, now that he is come to man's estate."

So she went to Ithaca, and there she took upon her the form of Mentor, who was chief of the Taphians.

Now there were gathered in the house of Ulysses many princes from the islands, suitors of the Queen Penelopé, for they said that Ulysses was dead, and that she should choose another husband. These were gathered together, and were sitting playing draughts and feasting. And Telemachus sat among them, vexed at heart, for they wasted his substance, neither was he master in his house. But when he saw the guest at the door, he rose from his place and welcomed him, and made him sit down, and commanded that they should give him food and wine. And when he had ended his meal, Telemachus asked him of his business.

Thereupon the false Mentor said, "My name is Mentor, and I am King of the Taphians, and I am sailing to Cyprus for copper, taking iron in exchange. Now I have been long time the friend of this house, of thy father and thy father's father, and I came trusting to see thy father, for they told me that he was here. But now I see that some god has hindered his return, for that he lives I know full well."

And after this the two had much talk together, and Athené gave good counsel to Telemachus, and chiefly that he should go to Pylos, to old Nestor, and to Sparta, where Menelaüs dwelt, if haply he might hear aught of his father in this place or in that. And after this she departed; and as she went, Telemachus knew her who she was.

The next day the people of Ithaca were called to an assembly. And Telemachus stood up among them and said—

"I have great trouble in my heart, men of Ithaca, for first my father is not, whom ye all loved; and next, the princes of the islands come hither, making suit to my mother, but she waits ever for her husband, when he shall return. And they devour all our substance, nor is Ulysses here to defend it, and I, in truth, am not able. And this is a grievous wrong, and not to be borne."

Then he dashed his sceptre on the ground, and sat down weeping. And Antinoüs, who was one of the suitors, rose up and said—

"Nay, Telemachus, blame not us, but blame thy mother, who indeed is crafty above all women. For now this is the fourth year that we have come suing for her hand, and she has cheated us with hopes. Hear now this that she did. She set up a great warp for weaving, and said to us, 'Listen, ye that are my suitors. Hasten not my marriage till I finish this web to be a burial cloth for Laertes, for indeed it would be foul shame if he who has won great possessions should lack this honour.' So she spake, and for three years she cheated us, for what she wove in the day she undid at night. But when the fourth year was come, one of her maidens told us of the matter, and we came upon her by night and found her undoing the web, even what she had woven in the day. Then did she finish it, much against her will. Send away, therefore, thy mother, and bid her marry whom she will. But till this be done we will not depart."

Then answered Telemachus, "How can I send her away against her will, who bare me and brought me up? Much forfeit must I pay to Icarus, her father; ay, and the curses of my mother would abide on me. Wherefore I cannot do this thing."

So he spake; and there came two eagles, which flew abreast till they came over the assembly. Then did they wheel in the air, and shook out from each many feathers, and tare each other, and so departed.

Then cried Alitherses, the soothsayer, "Beware, ye suitors, for great trouble is coming to you, and to others also. And as for Ulysses, I said when he went to Troy that he should return after twenty years; and so it shall be."

And when the suitors would not listen, Telemachus said, "Yet give me a ship and twenty rowers, that I may go to Pylos and to Sparta, if haply I may hear news of my father."

But this also they would not, and the assembly was dismissed.

But Telemachus went out to the sea-shore, and prayed to Athené that she would help him. And while he prayed, lo! she stood by him, having the shape of a certain Mentes, who indeed had spoken on his behalf in the assembly. And she said—

"Thou art not, I trow, without spirit and

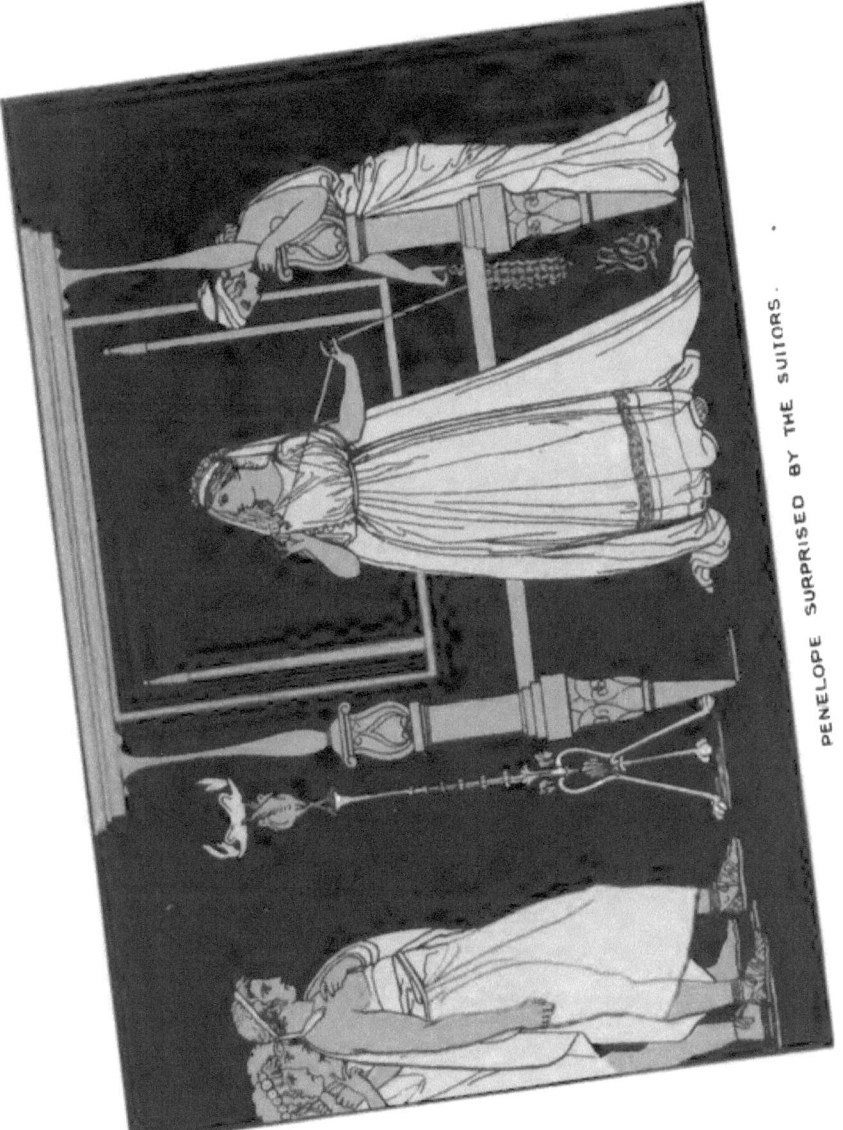

PENELOPE SURPRISED BY THE SUITORS.

wit, and art like to be a true son of Ulysses and Penelopé. Wherefore I have good hopes that this journey of which thou speakest will not be in vain. But as for the suitors, think not of them, for they lack wisdom, nor know the doom that is even now close upon them. Go, therefore, and talk with the suitors as before, and get ready meat for a journey, wine and meal. And I will gather men who will offer themselves freely for the journey, and find a ship also, the best in Ithaca."

Then Telemachus returned to the house. And Antinoüs caught him by the hand and said, " Eat and drink, Telemachus, and we will find a ship and rowers for thee, that thou mayest go where thou wilt, to inquire for thy father."

But Telemachus answered, "Think ye that I will eat and drink with you, who so shamefully waste my substance? Be sure of this, that I will seek vengeance against you, and if ye deny me a ship, I will even go with another man's."

So he spake, and dragged his hand from the hand of Antinoüs.

And another of the suitors said, "Now will Telemachus go and seek help against us from Pylos or from Sparta, or may be he will put poison in our cups, and so destroy us."

And another said, "Perchance he also will perish, as his father has perished. Then should we have much labour, even dividing all his substance, but the house should we give to his mother and to her husband."

So they spake, mocking him. But he went to the chamber of his father, in which were ranged many casks of old wine, and store of gold and bronze, and clothing and olive oil; and of these things the prudent Euryclea, who was the keeper of the house, had care. To her he spake, "Mother, make ready for me twelve jars of wine, not of the best, but of that which is next to it, and twenty measures of barley-meal. At even will I take them, when my mother sleeps, for I go to Pylos and Sparta, if perchance I may hear news of my father."

But the old woman said, weeping, "What meanest thou, being an only son, thus to travel abroad? Wilt thou perish, as thy father has perished? For this evil brood of suitors will devise means to slay thee and divide thy goods. Thou hadst better sit peaceably at home."

Then Telemachus said, "'Tis at the bidding of the gods I go. Only swear that thou wilt say nought to my mother till eleven or twelve days be past, unless perchance she should ask concerning me."

And the old woman sware that it should be so. And Telemachus went again among the suitors. But Athené, meanwhile, taking his shape, had gathered together a crew, and also had borrowed a ship for the voyage. And lest the suitors should hinder the thing, she caused a deep sleep to fall upon them, that they slept where they sat. Then she came in the shape of Mentor to the palace, and called Telemachus forth, saying, "The rowers are ready; let us go."

So they two went together and came to the ship. And they sat on the stern together, and the rowers sat upon the benches. Then Athené caused a west wind to blow, and they raised the mast and set the sail, and all night long the ship ran before the wind.

CHAPTER V.

NESTOR AND MENELAÜS.

IN the morning they came to Pylos. And lo! there was a great sacrifice to Poseidon on the shore, nine companies of men, and five hundred men in each company, and to each nine oxen. And Nestor was there with his sons; and when he saw the two travellers he bade them welcome, and caused them to sit down and to eat and drink, not forgetting to pour out of the wine to King Poseidon. And this they did, praying that he would help them in the matter whereon they had come from their home.

And when the feast was ended, Nestor asked them of their name and business. So Telemachus told him that he was come seeking news of his father Ulysses. And Nestor praised him much that he spake so wisely, but of his father he could tell him nothing, only that he had stayed a while at Troy to do pleasure to King Agamemnon. Diomed, he said, had returned safe, and he himself to Pylos, and the Myrmidons, with the son of Achilles, and Philoctetes also, and Idomeneus. And Menelaüs also had come back to his home, after wanderings many and great. But of Ulysses no one knew anything at all. Then they talked of many things, and specially of King Agamemnon, how he had been slain and also avenged.

And when evening was come, Athené indeed departed (and they knew her as she went for a goddess), but Telemachus remained, for he would go (for so Nestor advised) to Sparta, to inquire of King Menelaüs, being the latest returned of all the kings.

On the morrow Nestor held a sacrifice to Athené, and on the morrow after that Nestor bade his men yoke horses to a chariot, and Pisistratus, who was the youngest of his sons, took the reins, and Telemachus rode with him. And all that day they journeyed; and when the land grew dark they came to the city of Pheræ, where Diocles, son of Orsilochus, was king, and there they rested; and the next day, travelling again, came to Lacedæmon, to the palace of King Menelaüs.

And it chanced that Menelaüs had made a great feast that day, for his daughter Hermioné, the child of the fair Helen, was married to Neoptolemus, the son of Achilles, to whom she had been promised at Troy; and he had also taken a wife for his son Megapenthes. And the two stayed their chariot at the door, and one spied them, and said to Menelaüs—

"Lo! here are two strangers who are like the children of kings. Shall we keep them here, or send them to another?"

But Menelaüs was wroth, and said, "Shall we, who have eaten so often of the bread of hospitality, send these strangers to another? Nay, but unyoke their horses and bid them sit down to meat."

So the two lighted from the chariot, and after the bath they sat down to meat. And when they had ended the meal, Telemachus, looking round at the hall, said to his companion—

"See the gold and the amber, and the silver and the ivory. This is as the hall of Olympian Zeus."

This he spake with his face close to his comrade's ear, but Menelaüs heard him and said—

"With the halls of the gods nothing mortal may compare. And among men also there may be the match of these things. Yet I have wandered far, and got many possessions in many lands. But woe is me! while I gathered these things my brother was foully slain in his house. Would that I had but the third part of this wealth of mine, so that they who perished at Troy were alive again! And most of all I mourn for the great Ulysses, for whether he be alive or dead no man knows."

But Telemachus wept to hear mention of his father, holding up his purple cloak before his eyes. This Menelaüs saw, and knew him who he was, and pondered whether he should wait till he should himself speak of his father, or should rather ask him of his errand. But while he pondered there came in the fair Helen, and three maidens with her, of whom one set a couch for her to sit, and one spread a carpet for her feet, and one bare a basket of purple wool, but she herself had a distaff of gold in her hand. And when she saw the strangers she said—

"Who are these, Menelaüs? Never have I seen such likeness in man or woman as this one bears to Ulysses. Surely 'tis his son Telemachus, whom he left an infant at home when ye went to Troy for my sake!"

Then said Menelaüs, "It must indeed be so, lady. For these are the hands and feet of Ulysses, and the look of his eyes and his hair. And but now, when I made mention of his name, he wept."

Then said Pisistratus, "King Menelaüs, thou speakest truth. This is indeed the son of Ulysses, who is come to thee, if haply thou canst help him by word or deed."

And Menelaüs answered, "Then is he the son of a man whom I loved right well. I thought to give him a city in this land, bringing him from Ithaca with all his goods. Then might we often have companied together, nor should aught have divided us but death itself. But these things the gods have ordered otherwise."

At these words they all wept—the fair Helen

and Telemachus and Menelaüs; nor could Pisistratus refrain himself, for he thought of his dear brother Antilochus, whom Memnon, son of the Morning, slew at Troy. But the fair Helen put a mighty medicine in the wine whereof they drank—nepenthé men call it. So mighty is it that whosoever drinks of it, that day he weeps not, though father and mother die, and though men slay brother or son before his eyes. Polydamna, wife of King Thoas, had given it to her in Egypt, where indeed many medicines grow that are mighty both for good and ill.

And after this she said, " It were long to tell all the wise and valiant deeds of Ulysses. One thing, however, ye shall hear, and it is this: while the Greeks were before Troy he came into the city, having disguised himself as a beggar-man, yea, and he had laid many blows upon himself, so that he seemed to have been shamefully entreated. I only knew him who he was, and questioned him, but he answered craftily. And afterwards, when I had bathed him and anointed him with oil, I swore that I would not tell the thing till he had gone back to the camp. So he slew many Trojans with the sword, and learnt many things. And while other women in Troy lamented, I was glad, for my heart was turned again to my home."

Then Menelaüs said, "Thou speakest truly, lady. Many men have I seen, and travelled over many lands, but never have I seen one who might be matched with Ulysses. Well do I remember how, when I and other chiefs of the Greeks sat in the horse of wood, thou didst come, Deïphobus following thee. Some god who loved the sons of Troy put the thing into thy heart. Thrice didst thou walk round our hiding-place and call by name to each one of the chiefs, likening thy voice in marvellous fashion to the voice of his wife. Then would Diomed and I have either risen from our place or answered thee straightway. But Ulysses hindered us, so saving all the Greeks."

But Telemachus said, "Yet all these things have not kept him, but that he has perished."

And now it was the hour of sleep. And the next day Menelaüs asked Telemachus of his business.

Then Telemachus said, "I have come, if haply thou canst tell me aught of my father. For certain suitors of my mother devour my goods, nor do I see any help. Tell me therefore true, sparing me not at all, but saying if thou knowest anything of thyself, or hast heard it from another."

And Menelaüs answered, "It angers me to hear of these cowards who would lie in a brave man's bed. So a hind lays its young in a lion's den, but when he comes he slays both her and them. So shall it be with these in the day when Ulysses shall come back. But as to what thou askest me, I will answer clearly and without turning aside. I was in Egypt, the gods hindering my voyage because I had not offered due sacrifice. Now there is an island, Pharos men call it, a day's journey from the shore for a swift ship with a fair wind blowing. And in this I tarried against my will, the wind being contrary, ay, and should have died, but that Idothea, daughter of old Proteus, had pity on me. For she found me sitting alone while my companions fished with hooks, for hunger pressed them sore. And she said, 'Art thou altogether a fool, stranger, and without spirit, that thou sittest thus helpless, and seekest no deliverance, while the hearts of thy companions faint within them?' And I said, 'I tarry here against my will, for some god hinders my voyage, and thou, if thou be of the immortals, canst tell me whom I have offended.' Then she made answer, 'There is an old man of the sea who knows all things: his name is Proteus, and he is my father. And if thou couldst lie in ambush and take him, he would tell thee how thou mayest return to thy home, ay, and tell thee all, be it good or evil, that has befallen thee there.' And when I would fain know how I might lie in ambush and take him, seeing that it was hard for a mortal to master a god, she said, 'At noonday he comes to sleep in his caves, and his herd of seals comes with him. Thou must take three of thy companions whom thou judgest to be bravest, and I will hide you. Now the old man counts the seals, and when he has told the number he lies down in the midst. Then take heart and rush upon him, thou and thy companions. Much will he try to escape, making himself into all kinds of moving things, and into water and into fire. But when he shall ask of thy errand, being such in shape as thou sawest him lie down, then may ye loose him, and he will tell thee what thou wouldst know.' The next day came Idothea, bringing with her the skins of four seals which she had newly slain. Holes she made in the sand of the sea, and bade us sit in them, putting upon us the skins. It would have been a dreadful ambush for us, so evil was the smell of the seals, but the goddess gave us ambrosia, that we might hold under our nostrils, and the sweet savour prevailed against the smell. And at noon the old man came and counted the seals, and lay down to sleep. Then we rushed upon him; and the old man made himself now a lion, and now a snake and a leopard and a boar, and after this water, and then a tree in leaf. But still we held him. And at the last he asked me what I would. So I told him. And he said that I must first return over the sea to Egypt, and make due offerings to the gods. And when he had said this, I asked him of the chiefs, my friends, whether they had come back safe from Troy. And he said, 'Two only of the chiefs have perished; but those that fell in battle thou knowest thyself. Ajax, son of Oileus, was shipwrecked, and yet might have lived, but he spake blasphemously, so that Poseidon smote the rock whereon he sat, and he drank the salt water and perished. And thy brother Agamemnon was slain at a feast by the false Ægisthus.' Then I said, 'There is yet another of whom I would hear.' And he answered, 'I saw the son of Laertes weeping in the island of Calypso, who keeps him against his will, nor can he depart, having neither ship nor rowers.' And after this the old man departed, and I, when I had done that which was commanded, and had made a great tomb for Agamemnon, my brother, came back hither. And now I would that thou shouldest stay here awhile, and I will give thee horses and a chariot, and a cup from which thou mayest pour out wine to the gods."

Then Telemachus answered, "I thank thee for the horses, but we may not keep such beasts in Ithaca, for it is rocky, and fit only for pasturing of goats."

And Menelaüs said, smiling, "Thou speakest well and wisely; but at least I will give thee other things, many and seemly, instead of the horses."

Now it had been made known meanwhile to

the suitors in Ithaca that Telemachus was gone upon this journey seeking his father, and the thing displeased them much. And after that they had held counsel about the matter, it seemed best that they should lay an ambush against him, which should slay him as he came back to his home. So Antinoüs took twenty men and departed, purposing to lie in wait in the strait between Ithaca and Samos.

Nor was this counsel unknown to Penelopé, for the herald Medon had heard it, and he told her how that Telemachus had gone seeking news of his father, and how the suitors purposed to slay him as he returned. And she called her women, old and young, and rebuked them, saying, "Wicked that ye were, that knew that he was about to go, and did not rouse me from my bed. Surely I had kept him, eager though he was, from his journey, or he had left me dead behind him!"

Then said Euryclea, "Slay me, if thou wilt, but I will hide nothing from thee. I knew his purpose, and I furnished him with such things as he needed. But he made me swear that I would not tell thee till the eleventh or the twelfth day was come. But go with thy maidens and make thy prayer to Athené that she will save him from death; and indeed I think that this house is not altogether hated by the gods."

Then Penelopé, having duly prepared herself, went with her maidens to the upper chamber, and prayed aloud to Athené that she would save her son. And the suitors heard her praying, and said, "Surely the queen prays, thinking of her marriage, nor knows that death is near to her son."

Then she lay down to sleep, and had neither eaten nor drunk. And while she slept Athené sent her a dream in the likeness of her sister Iphthimé, who was the wife of Eumelus, son of Alcestis. And the vision stood over her head and spake, "Sleepest thou, Penelopé? The gods would not have thee grieve, for thy son shall surely return."

And Penelopé said, "How camest thou here, my sister? For thy dwelling is far away. And how can I cease to weep when my husband is lost? And now my son is gone, and I am sore afraid for him, lest his enemies slay him."

PENELOPE'S DREAM

But the vision answered, "Fear not at all; for there is a mighty helper with him, even Athené, who has bid me tell thee these things."

Then Penelopé said, "If thou art a goddess, tell me this. Is my husband yet alive?"

But the vision answered, "That I cannot say, whether he be alive or dead." And so saying, it vanished into air.

And Penelopé woke from her sleep, and her heart was comforted.

CHAPTER VI.

ULYSSES ON HIS RAFT.

WHILE Telemachus was yet sojourning in Sparta, Zeus sent Hermes to Calypso, to bid her that she should let Ulysses go. So Hermes donned his golden sandals, and took his wand in his hand, and came to the island of Ogygia, and to the cave where Calypso dwelt. A fair place it was. In the cave was burning a fire of sweet-smelling wood, and Calypso sat at her loom and sang with a lovely voice. And round about the cave was a grove of alders and poplars and cypresses, wherein many birds, falcons and owls and sea-crows, were wont to roost; and all about the mouth of the cave was a vine with purple clusters of grapes; and there were four fountains which streamed four ways through meadows of parsley and violet. But Ulysses was not there, for he sat, as was his wont, on the sea-shore, weeping and groaning because he might not see wife and home and country.

And Calypso spied Hermes, and bade him come within, and gave him meat and drink, ambrosia and nectar, which are the food of the gods. And when he had ended his meal, she asked him of his errand. So he told her that he was come, at the bidding of Zeus, in the matter of Ulysses, for that it was the pleasure of the gods that he should return to his native country, and that she should not hinder him any more. It vexed Calypso much to hear this, for she would fain have kept Ulysses with her always, and she said—

" Ye gods are always jealous when a goddess loves a mortal man. And as for Ulysses, did not I save him when Zeus had smitten his ship with a thunderbolt, and all his comrades had perished? And now let him go—if it pleases Zeus. Only I cannot send him, for I have neither ship nor rowers. Yet will I willingly teach him how he may safely return."

And Hermes said, " Do this thing speedily, lest Zeus be wroth with thee."

So he departed. And Calypso went seeking

Ulysses, and found him on the shore of the sea, looking out over the waters, as was his wont, and weeping, for he was weary of his life, so much did he desire to see Ithaca again. She stood by him and said—

"Weary not for thy native country, nor waste thyself with tears. If thou wilt go, I will speed thee on thy way. Take therefore thine axe and cut thee beams, and join them together, and make a deck upon them, and I will give thee bread and water and wine, and clothe thee also, so that thou mayest return safe to thy native country, for the gods will have it so."

"Nay," said Ulysses, "what is this that thou sayest? Shall I pass in a raft over the dreadful sea, over which even ships go not without harm? I will not go against thy will; but thou must swear the great oath of the gods that thou plannest no evil against me."

Then Calypso smiled and said, "These are strange words. By the Styx I swear that I plan no harm against thee, but only such good as I would ask myself, did I need it; for indeed my heart is not of iron, but rather full of compassion."

Then they two went to the cave and sat down to meat, and she set before him food such as mortal men eat, but she herself ate ambrosia and drank nectar, as the gods are wont. And afterwards she said—

"Why art thou so eager for thy home? Surely if thou knewest all the trouble that awaits thee, thou wouldst not go, but wouldst rather dwell with me. And though thou desirest all the day long to see thy wife, surely I am not less fair than she."

"Be not angry," Ulysses made reply. "The wise Penelopé cannot indeed be compared to thee, for she is a mortal woman and thou art a goddess. Yet is my home dear to me, and I would fain see it again."

The next day Calypso gave him an axe with a handle of olive wood, and an adze, and took him to the end of the island, where there were great trees, long ago sapless and dry, alder and poplar and pine. Of these he felled twenty, and lopped them, and worked them by the line. Then the goddess brought him a gimlet, and he made holes in the logs and joined them with pegs. And he made decks and side-planking also; also a mast and a yard, and a rudder wherewith to turn the raft. And he fenced it about with a bulwark of osier against the waves. The sails, indeed, Calypso wove, and Ulysses fitted them with braces and halyards and sheets. And afterwards, with ropes, he moored the raft to the shore.

On the fourth day all was finished, and on the fifth day he departed. And Calypso gave him goodly garments, and a skin of wine, and a skin of water, and rich provender in a wallet of leather. She sent also a fair wind blowing behind, and Ulysses set his sails and proceeded joyfully on his way; nor did he sleep, but watched the sun and the stars, still steering, as indeed Calypso had bidden, to the left. So he sailed for seventeen days, and on the eighteenth he saw the hills of Phæacia and the land, which had the shape of a shield.

But Poseidon spied him as he sailed, and was wroth to see him so near to the end of his troubles. Wherefore he sent all the winds of heaven down upon him. Sore troubled was Ulysses, and said to himself, " It was truth that Calypso spake when she said how that I should suffer many troubles returning to my home. Would that I had died that day when many a spear was cast by the men of Troy over the dead Achilles. Then would the Greeks have buried me; but now shall I perish miserably."

And as he spake a great wave struck the raft and tossed him far away, so that he dropped the rudder from his hand. Nor for a long time could he rise, so deep was he sunk, and so heavy was the goodly clothing which Calypso had given him. Yet at the last he rose, and spat the salt water out of his mouth, and, so brave was he, sprang at the raft and caught it and sat thereon, and was borne hither and thither by the waves. But Ino saw him and pitied him—a woman she had been, and was now a goddess of the sea—and came and sat upon the waves, saying—

"Luckless mortal, why doth Poseidon hate thee so? He shall not slay thee, though he fain would do it. Put off these garments and swim to the land of Phæacia, putting this veil under thy breast. And when thou art come to the land, loose it from thee, and cast it into the sea; but when thou castest it, look away."

But Ulysses doubted what this might be, and thought that he would yet stay on the raft while the timbers held together, for that the land was far away. But as he thought, yet another great wave struck it, and scattered the timbers. And he sat upon one of them, as a man sits upon a horse; and then he stripped off the garments which Calypso had given him, and so, leaping into the sea, made to swim to the land.

And Poseidon saw him, and said, "Get to the shore if thou canst, but even so thou art not come to the end of thy troubles."

So for two days and two nights he swam, Athené helping him, for otherwise he had perished. But on the third day there was a calm, and he saw the land from the top of a great wave, for the waves were yet high, close at hand. Dear as a father to his son, rising up from grievous sickness, so dear was the land to Ulysses. But when he came near he heard the waves breaking along the shore, for there was no harbour there, but only cliffs and rugged rocks. And while he doubted what he should do, a great wave bore him to the shore. Then would he have perished, all his bones being broken; but Athené put it in his heart to lay hold of a great rock till the wave had spent itself. And even then had he died, for the ebb caught him and bore him far out to sea; but he bethought him that he would swim along, if haply he might see some landing-place. And at last he came to the mouth of a river, where there were no rocks. Then at last he won his way to the land. His knees were bent under him and his hands dropped at his side, and the salt water ran out of his mouth and nostrils. Breathless was he, and speechless; but when he came to himself, he loosed the veil from under his breast and cast it into the sea.

Then he lay down on the rushes by the bank of the river and kissed the earth, thinking within himself, "What now shall I do? for if I sleep here by the river, I fear that the dew and the frost may slay me: for indeed in the morning-time the wind from the river blows cold. And if I go up to the wood, to lay me down to sleep in the thicket, I fear that some evil beast may devour me."

But it seemed better to go to the wood. So

he went. Now this was close to the river, and he found two bushes, of wild olive one, and of fruitful olive the other. So thickly grown together were they, that the winds blew not through them, nor did the sun pierce them, nor yet the rain. Thereunder crept Ulysses, and found great store of leaves, shelter enough for two or three, even in a great storm. Then, even as a man who dwells apart from others cherishes his fire, hiding it under the ashes, so Ulysses cherished his life under the leaves. And Athené sent down upon his eyelids deep sleep, that might ease him of his toil.

CHAPTER VII.

NAUSICAA AND ALCINOÜS.

Now the king of Phæacia was Alcinoüs, and he had five sons and one daughter, Nausicaa. To her, where she slept with her two maidens by her, Athené went, taking the shape of her friend, the daughter of Dymas, and said—

"Why hath thy mother so idle a daughter, Nausicaa? Lo! thy garments lie unwashed, and thy wedding must be near, seeing that many nobles in the land are suitors to thee. Ask then thy father that he give thee the waggon with the mules, for the laundries are far from the city, and I will go with thee."

And when the morning was come, Nausicaa awoke, marvelling at the dream, and went seeking her parents. Her mother she found busy with her maidens at the loom, and her father she met as he was going to the council with the chiefs of the land. Then she said, "Give me, father, the waggon with the mules, that I may take the garments to the river to wash them. Thou shouldest always have clean robes when thou goest to the council; and there are my five brothers also, who love to have newly washed garments at the dance."

But of her own marriage she said nothing. And her father, knowing her thoughts, said, "It is well. The men shall harness the waggon for thee."

So they put the clothing into the waggon. And her mother put also food and wine, and olive oil also, wherewith she and her maidens might anoint themselves after the bath. So they climbed into the waggon and went to the river. And then they washed the clothing, and spread it out to dry on the rocks by the sea. And after that they had bathed and anointed themselves, they sat down to eat and drink by the river side; and after the meal they played at ball, singing as they played, and Nausicaa, fair as Artemis when she hunts on Taygetus or Erymanthus wild goats and stags, led the song. But when they had nearly ended their play, the princess, throwing the ball to one of her maidens, cast it so wide that it fell into the river. Whereupon they all cried aloud, and Ulysses awoke. And he said to himself, "What is this land to which I have come? Are they that dwell therein fierce or kind to strangers? Just now I seemed to hear the voice of nymphs, or am I near the dwellings of men?"

Then he twisted leaves about his loins, and rose up and went towards the maidens, who indeed were frighted to see him (for he was wild of aspect), and fled hither and thither. But Nausicaa stood and fled not. Then Ulysses thought within himself, should he go near and clasp her knees, or, lest haply this should anger her, should he stand and speak? And this he did, saying—

"I am thy suppliant, O queen. Whether thou art a goddess, I know not. But if thou art a mortal, happy thy father and mother, and happy thy brothers, and happiest of all he who shall win thee in marriage. Never have I seen man or woman so fair. Thou art like a young palm-tree that but lately I saw in Delos, springing by the temple of the god. But as for me,

I have been cast on this shore, having come from the island Ogygia. Pity me, then, and lead me to the city, and give me something, a wrapper of this linen, maybe, to put about me. So may the gods give thee all blessings!"

And Nausicaa made answer, "Thou seemest, stranger, to be neither evil nor foolish; and as for thy plight, the gods give good fortune or bad, as they will. Thou shalt not lack clothing or food, or anything that a suppliant should have. And I will take thee to the city. Know also that this land is Phæacia, and that I am daughter to Alcinoüs, who is king thereof."

Then she called to her maidens, "What mean ye, to flee when ye see a man? No enemy comes hither to harm us, for we are dear to the gods, and also we live in an island of the sea, so that men may not approach to work us wrong; but if one cometh here overborne by trouble, it is well to succour him. Give this man, therefore, food and drink, and wash him in the river, where there is shelter from the wind."

So they brought him down to the river, and gave him a tunic and a cloak to clothe himself withal, and also oil-olive in a flask of gold. Then, at his bidding, they departed a little space, and he washed the salt from his skin and out of his hair, and anointed himself, and put on the clothing. And Athené made him taller and fairer to see, and caused the hair to be thick on his head, in colour as a hyacinth. Then he sat down on the sea-shore, right beautiful to behold, and the maiden said—

"Not without some bidding of the gods comes this man to our land. Before, indeed, I deemed him uncomely, but now he seems like to the gods. I should be well content to have such a man for a husband, and maybe he might will to abide in this land. But give him, ye maidens, food and drink."

So they gave him, and he ate ravenously, having fasted long. Then Nausicaa bade yoke the mules, and said to Ulysses—

"Follow thou with the maidens, and I will lead the way in the waggon. For I would not that the people should speak lightly of me. And I doubt not that were thou with me some one of the baser sort would say, 'Who is this stranger, tall and fair, that cometh with

Nausicaa? Will he be her husband? Perchance it is some god who has come down at her prayer, or a man from far away; for of us men of Phæacia she thinks scorn.' It would be shame that such words should be spoken. And indeed it is ill-done of a maiden who, father and mother unknowing, companies with men. Do thou, then, follow behind, and when we are come to the city, tarry in a poplar grove that thou shalt see ('tis the grove of Athené) till I shall have come to my father's house. Then follow; and for the house, that any one, even a child, can show thee, for the other Phæacians dwell not in such. And when thou art come within the doors, pass quickly throu ghthe hall to where my mother sits. Close to the hearth is her seat, and my father's hard by, where he sits with the wine cup in his hand, as a god. Pass him by and lay hold of her knees, and pray her that she give thee safe return to thy country."

It was evening when they came to the city. And Nausicaa drove the waggon to the palace. Then her brothers came out to her, and loosed the mules and carried in the clothing. Then

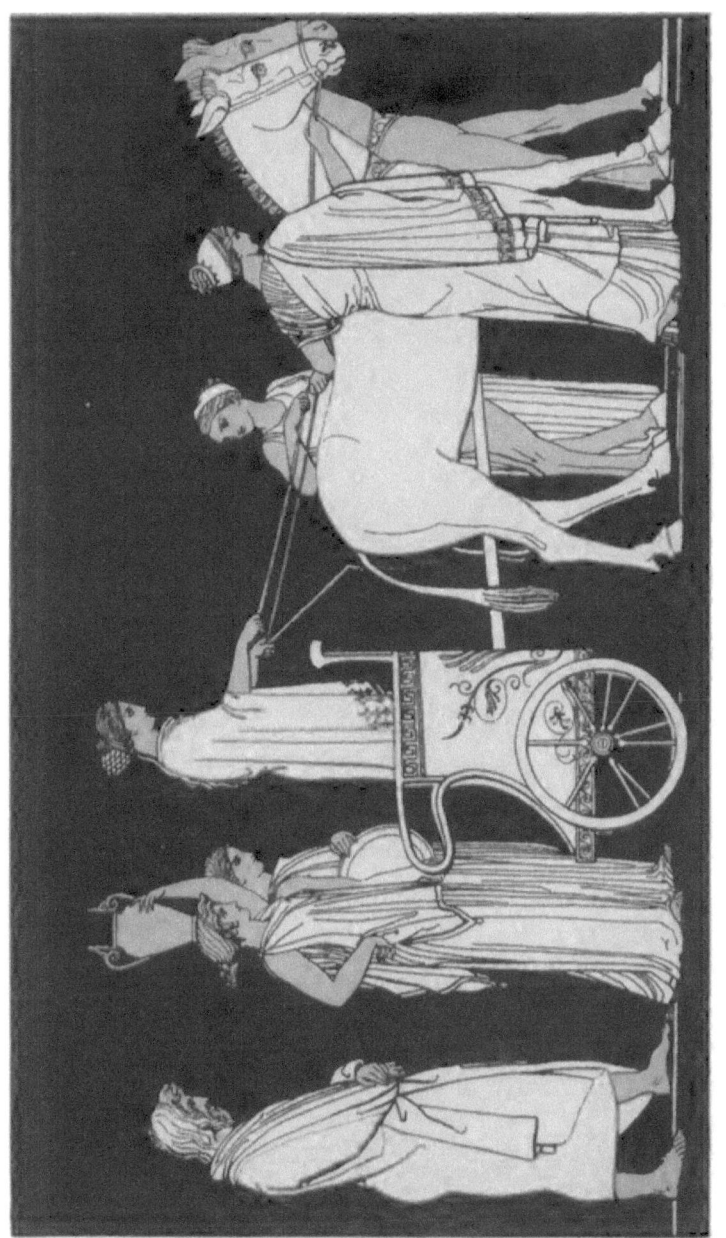

ULYSSES FOLLOWING THE CAR OF NAUSICAA.

she went to her chamber, where Eurymedusa, who was her nurse, lighted a fire and prepared a meal. Meanwhile Ulysses came from the grove, and lest any one should see him, Athené spread a mist about him, and when he had now reached the city, she took the shape of a young maiden carrying a pitcher, and met him.

Then Ulysses asked her, "My child, canst thou tell me where dwells Alcinoüs? for I am a stranger in this place."

And she answered, "I will show thee, for indeed he dwells nigh to my own father. But be thou silent, for we Phæacians love not strangers over much." Then she led him to the palace. A wondrous place it was, with walls of brass and doors of gold, hanging on posts of silver; and on either side of the door were dogs of gold and silver, the work of Hephæstus, and against the wall, all along from the threshold to the inner chamber, were set seats, on which sat the chiefs of the Phæacians, feasting; and youths wrought in gold stood holding torches in their hands, to give light in the darkness. Fifty women were in the house grinding corn and weaving robes, for the women of the land are no less skilled to weave than are the men to sail the sea. And round about the house were gardens beautiful exceedingly, with orchards of fig, and apple, and pear, and pomegranate, and olive. Drought hurts them not, nor frost, and harvest comes after harvest without ceasing. Also there was a vineyard; and some of the grapes were parching in the sun, and some were being gathered, and some again were but just turning red. And there were beds of all manner of flowers; and in the midst of all were two fountains which never failed.

These things Ulysses regarded for a space, and then passed into the hall. And there the chiefs of Phæacia were drinking their last cup to Hermes. Quickly he passed through them, and put his hands on the knees of Areté and said—and as he spake the mist cleared from about him, and all that were in the hall beheld him—

"I am a suppliant to thee, and to thy husband, and to thy guests. The gods bless thee and them, and grant you to live in peace, and that your children should come peacefully after you. Only, do you send me home to my native country."

And he sat down in the ashes of the hearth. Then for a space all were silent, but at the last spake Echeneüs, who was the oldest man in the land—

"King Alcinoüs, this ill becomes you that this man should sit in the ashes of the hearth. Raise him and bid him sit upon a seat, and let us pour out to Father Zeus, who is the friend of suppliants, and let the keeper of the house give him meat and drink."

And Alcinoüs did so, bidding his eldest born, Laodamas, rise from his seat. And an attendant poured water on his hands, and the keeper of the house gave him meat and drink. Then, when all had poured out to Father Zeus, King Alcinoüs said that they would take counsel on the morrow about sending this stranger to his home. And they answered that it should be so, and went each to his home. Only Ulysses was left in the hall, and Alcinoüs and Areté with him. And Areté saw his cloak and tunic, that she and her maidens had made them, and said—

"Whence art thou, stranger? and who gave thee these garments?"

So Ulysses told her how he had come from the island of Calypso, and what he had suffered, and how Nausicaa had found him on the shore, and had guided him to the city.

But Alcinoüs blamed the maiden that she had not herself brought him to the house. "For thou wast her suppliant," he said.

"Nay," said Ulysses; "she would have brought me, but I would not, fearing thy wrath." For he would not have the maiden blamed.

Then said Alcinoüs, "I am not one to be angered for such cause. Gladly would I have such a one as thou art to be my son-in-law, and I would give him house and wealth. But no one would I stay against his will. And as for sending thee to thy home, that is easy; for thou shalt sleep, and they shall take thee meanwhile."

And after this they slept. And the next day the king called the chiefs to an assembly, and told them of his purpose, that he would send this stranger to his home, for that it was their wont to show such kindness to such as needed it. And he bade fifty and two of the younger men make ready a ship, and that the elders should come to his house, and bring Demodocus, the minstrel, with them, for that he was minded to make a great feast for this stranger before he departed. So the youths made ready the ship. And afterwards there were gathered together a great multitude, so that the palace was filled from the one end to the other. And Alcinoüs slew for them twelve sheep and eight swine and two oxen. And when they had feasted to the full, the minstrel sang to them of how Achilles and Ulysses had striven together with fierce words at a feast, and how King Agamemnon was glad, seeing that so the prophecy of Apollo was fulfilled, saying that when valour and counsel should fall out, the end of Troy should come. But when Ulysses heard the song, he wept, holding his mantle before his face.

This Alcinoüs perceived, and said to the chiefs, " Now that we have feasted and delighted ourselves with song, let us go forth, that this stranger may see that we are skilful in boxing and wrestling and running."

So they went forth, a herald leading Demodocus by the hand, for the minstrel was blind. Then stood up many Phæacian youths, and the fairest and strongest of them all was Laodamas, eldest son to the king, and after him Euryalus. And next they ran a race, and Clytoneus was the swiftest. And among the wrestlers Euryalus was the best, and of the boxers, Laodamas. And in throwing the quoit Elatrius excelled, and in leaping at the bar, Amphialus.

Then Laodamas, Euryalus urging him, said to Ulysses, "Father, wilt thou not try thy skill in some game, and put away the trouble from thy heart?"

But Ulysses answered, "Why askest thou this? I think of my troubles rather than of sport, and sit among you, caring only that I may see again my home."

Then said Euryalus, "And in very truth, stranger, thou hast not the look of a wrestler or boxer. Rather would one judge thee to be some trader, who sails over the sea for gain."

"Nay," answered Ulysses, "this is ill said. So true is it that the gods give not all gifts to all men, beauty to one and sweet speech to

ULYSSES WEEPS AT THE SONG OF DEMODOCUS.

another. Fair of form art thou, no god could better thee; but thou speakest idle words. I am not unskilled in these things, but stood among the first in the old days; but since have I suffered much in battle and shipwreck. Yet will I make trial of my strength, for thy words have angered me."

Whereupon he took a quoit, heavier far than such as the Phæacians were wont to throw, and sent it with a whirl. It hurtled through the air, so that the brave Phæacians crouched to the ground in fear, and fell far beyond all the rest.

Then said Ulysses, "Come now, I will contend in wrestling or boxing, or even in the race, with any man in Phæacia, save Laodamas only, for he is my friend. I can shoot with the bow, and only Philoctetes could surpass me; and I can cast a spear as far as other men can shoot an arrow. But as for the race, it may be that some one might outrun me, for I have suffered much on the sea."

But they all were silent, till the king stood up and said, "Thou hast spoken well. But we men of Phæacia are not mighty to wrestle or to box; only we are swift of foot, and skilful to sail upon the sea. And we love feasts, and dances, and the harp, and gay clothing, and the bath. In these things no man may surpass us."

Then the king bade Demodocus the minstrel sing again. And when he had done so, the king's two sons, Alius and Laodamas, danced together; and afterwards they played with the ball, throwing it into the air, cloud high, and catching it right skilfully.

And afterwards the king said, "Let us each give this stranger a mantle and a tunic and a talent of gold, and let Euryalus make his peace with words and with a gift."

And they all (now there were twelve princes, and Alcinoüs the thirteenth) said that it should be so; also Euryalus gave Ulysses a sword with a hilt of silver and a scabbard of ivory. And after this Ulysses went to the bath, and then they all sat down to the feast. But as he went to the hall, Nausicaa, fair as a goddess, met him and said—

"Hail, stranger; thou wilt remember me in thy native country, for thou owest me thanks for thy life."

And he answered, "Every day in my native country will I remember thee, for indeed, fair maiden, thou didst save my life."

And when they were set down to the feast, Ulysses sent a portion of the chine which the king had caused to be set before him to the minstrel Demodocus, with a message that he should sing to them of the horse of wood which Epeius made, Athené helping him, and how Ulysses brought it into Troy, full of men of war who should destroy the city.

Then the minstrel sang how that some of the Greeks sailed away, having set fire to their tents, and some hid themselves in the horse with Ulysses, and how the men of Troy sat around, taking counsel what they should do with it, and some judged that they should rip it open, and some that they should throw it from the hill-top, and others again that they should leave it to be a peace-offering to the gods; and how the Greeks issued forth from their lurking-place and spoiled the city, and how Ulysses and Menelaüs went to the house of Deïphobus.

So he sang, and Ulysses wept to hear the tale. And when Alcinoüs perceived that he wept, he bade Demodocus cease from his song, for that some that were there liked it not. And to Ulysses he said that he should tell them who was his father and his mother, and from what land he came, and what was his name. All these things Ulysses told them, and all that he had done and suffered, down to the time when the Princess Nausicaa found him on the river shore. And when he had ended, King Alcinoüs bade that the princes should give Ulysses yet other gifts; and after that they went each man to his house to sleep.

The next day King Alcinoüs put all the gifts into the ship. And when the evening was come Ulysses bade farewell to the king and to the queen, and departed.

CHAPTER VIII.

ULYSSES AND THE SWINEHERD.

Now Ulysses slept while the ship was sailing to Ithaca. And when it was come to the shore he yet slept. Wherefore the men lifted him out, and put him on the shore with all his goods that the princes of the Phæacians had given him, and so left him. After a while he awoke, and knew not the land, for there was a great mist about him, Athené having contrived that it should be so, for good ends, as will be seen. Very wroth was he with the men of Phæacia, thinking that they had cheated him; nor did it comfort him when he counted his goods to find that of these he had lost nothing.

But as he walked by the sea, lamenting his fate, Athené met him, having the shape of a young shepherd, fair to look upon, such as are the sons of kings; and Ulysses, when he saw him, was glad, and asked him how men called the country wherein he was.

And the false shepherd said, "Thou art foolish, or, may be, hast come from very far, not to know this country. Many men know it, both in the east and in the west. Rocky it is, not fit for horses, nor is it very broad; but it is fertile land, and full of wine; nor does it want for rain, and a good pasture it is for oxen and goats; and men call it Ithaca. Even in Troy, which is very far, they say, from this land of Greece, men have heard of Ithaca."

This Ulysses was right glad to hear. Yet he was not minded to say who he was, but rather to feign a tale.

So he said, "Yes, of a truth, I heard of this Ithaca in Crete, from which I am newly come with all this wealth, leaving also as much behind for my children. For I slew Orsilochus, son of Idomeneus the king, because he would have taken from me my spoil. Wherefore I slew him, lying in wait for him by the way. Then made I covenant with certain Phœnicians that they should take me to Pylos or to Elis; which thing indeed they were minded to do, only the wind

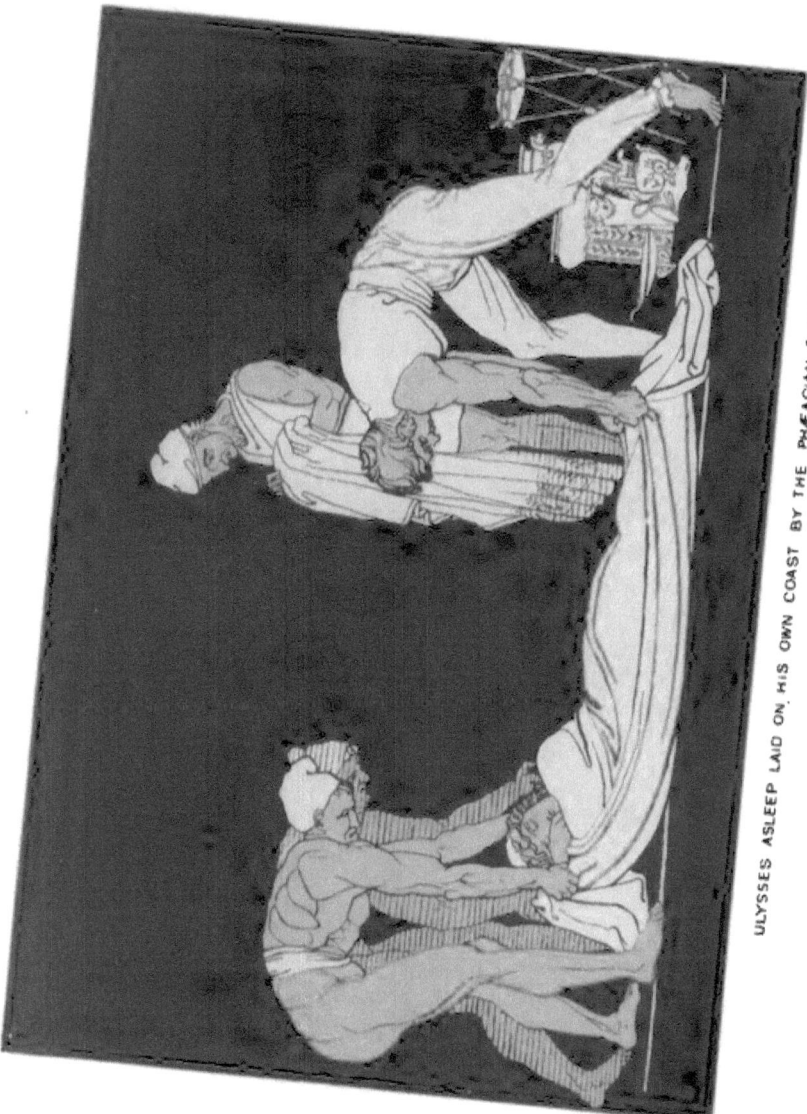

ULYSSES ASLEEP LAID ON HIS OWN COAST BY THE PHÆACIAN SAILORS.

drave them hither, and while I slept they put me upon the shore, and my possessions with me, and departed to Sidon."

This pleased Athené much, and she changed her shape, becoming like a woman, tall and fair, and said to Ulysses—

"Right cunning would he be who could cheat thee. Even now in thy native country ceasest thou not from cunning words and deceits! But let these things be; for thou, I trow, art the wisest of mortal men, and I excel among the gods in counsel. For I am Athené, daughter of Zeus, who am ever wont to stand by thee and help thee. And now we will hide these possessions of thine; and thou must be silent, nor tell to any one who thou art, and endure many things, so that thou mayest come to thine own again."

But still Ulysses doubted, and would have the goddess tell him whether of a truth he had come back to his native land. And she, commending his prudence, scattered the mist that was about him.

Then Ulysses knew the land, and kissed the ground, and prayed to the Nymphs that they would be favourable to him. And after this,

Athené guiding him, he hid away his possessions in a cave, and put a great stone on the mouth. Then the two took counsel together.

And Athené said, "Think, man of many devices, how thou wilt lay hands on these men, suitors of thy wife, who for three years have sat in thy house devouring thy substance. And she hath answered them craftily, making many promises, but still waiting for thy coming."

Then Ulysses said, "Truly I had perished, even as Agamemnon perished, but for thee. But do thou help me, as of old in Troy, for with thee at my side I would fight with three hundred men."

Then said Athené, "Lo! I will cause that no man shall know thee, for I will wither the fair flesh on thy limbs, and take the bright hair from thy head, and make thine eyes dull. And the suitors shall take no account of thee, neither shall thy wife nor thy son know thee. But go to the swineherd Eumæus, where he dwells by the fountain of Arethusa, for he is faithful to thee and to thy house. And I will hasten to Sparta, to the house of Menelaüs, to fetch Telemachus, for he went thither, seeking news of thee."

Then Athené changed him into the shape of a beggar-man. She caused his skin to wither, and his hair to fall off, and his eyes to grow dim, and put on him filthy rags, with a great stag's hide about his shoulders, and in his hand a staff, and a wallet on his shoulder, fastened by a rope.

Then she departed, and Ulysses went to the house of Eumæus, the swineherd. A great courtyard there was, and twelve sties for the sows, and four watchdogs, big as wild beasts, for such did the swineherd breed. He himself was shaping sandals, and of his men three were with the swine in the fields, and one was driving a fat beast to the city, to be meat for the suitors. But when Ulysses came near, the dogs ran upon him, and he dropped his staff and sat down, and yet would have suffered harm, even on his own threshold; but the swineherd ran forth and drave away the dogs, and brought the old man in, and gave him a seat of brushwood, with a great goat-skin over it.

And Ulysses said, "Zeus and the other gods requite thee for this kindness."

Then the two talked of matters in Ithaca, and Eumæus told how the suitors of the queen were devouring the substance of Ulysses. Then the false beggar asked him of the king, saying that perchance, having travelled far, he might know such an one.

But Eumæus said, "Nay, old man, thus do all wayfarers talk, yet we hear no truth from them. Not a vagabond fellow comes to this island but our queen must see him, and ask him many things, weeping the while. And thou, I doubt not, for a cloak or a tunic, would tell a wondrous tale. But Ulysses, I know, is dead, and either the fowls of the air devour him or the fishes of the sea."

And when the false beggar would have comforted him, saying he knew of a truth that Ulysses would yet return, he hearkened not. Moreover, he prophesied evil for Telemachus also, who had gone to seek news of his father, but would surely be slain by the suitors, who were even now lying in wait for him as he should return. And after this he asked the stranger who he was and whence he had come. Then Ulysses answered him craftily—

"I am a Cretan, the son of one Castor, by a slave woman. Now my father, while he lived, did

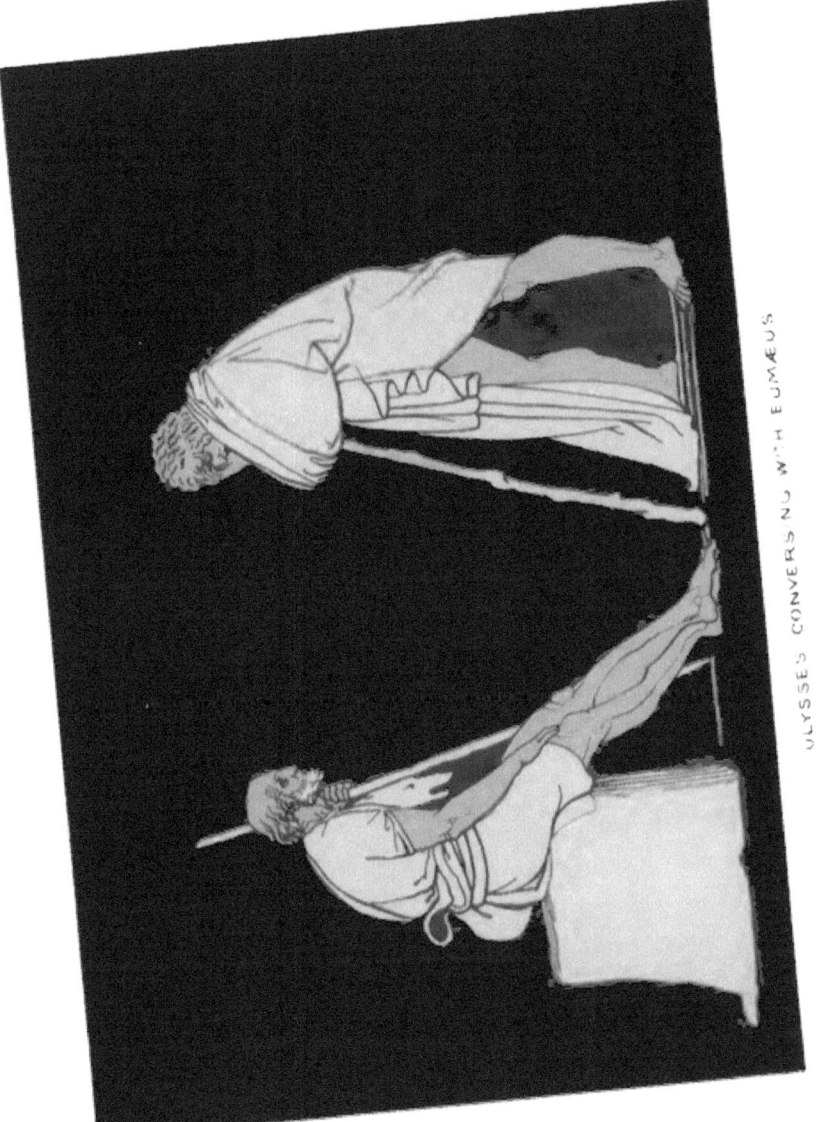

ULYSSES CONVERSING WITH EUMAEUS

by me as by his other sons. But when he died they divided his goods, and gave me but a small portion, and took my dwelling from me. Yet I won a rich wife for myself, for I was brave and of good repute. No man would sooner go to battle or to ambush than I, and I loved ships and spears and arrows, which some men hate, I trow. Nine times did I lead my followers in ships against strangers, and the tenth time I went with King Idomeneus to Troy. And when the city of Priam had perished, I went back to my native country, and there for the space of one month I tarried with my wife, and afterwards I sailed with nine ships to Egypt. On the fifth day—for the gods gave us a prosperous voyage—we came to the river of Egypt. There did my comrades work much wrong to the people of the land, spoiling their fields, and leading into captivity their wives and children; nor would they hearken to me when I would have stayed them. Then the Egyptians gathered an army, and came upon them, and slew some and took others. And I, throwing down helmet and spear and shield, hasted to the king of the land where he sat in his chariot, and prayed that he would have mercy on me, which thing he did. And with him I dwelt for seven years, gathering much wealth. But in the eighth year there came a trader of Phœnicia, who beguiled me, that I went with him to his country. And there I tarried for a year; and afterwards he carried me in his ship to Libya, meaning to sell me as a slave, but Zeus brake the ship, so that I only was left alive. Nine days did I float, keeping hold of the mast, and on the tenth a wave cast me on the land of Thresprotia, where King Pheidon kindly entreated me, giving me food and raiment. There did I hear tell of Ulysses; yea, and saw the riches which he had gathered together, which King Pheidon was keeping till he himself should come back from Dodona, from the oracle of Zeus. Thence I sailed in a ship for Dulichium, purposing to go to King Acastus, but the sailors were minded to sell me for a slave. Therefore they left me bound in the ship, but themselves took their supper on the shore. But in the meanwhile I brake my bonds, the gods helping me, and leaping into the sea, swam to the land, and hid myself in a wood that was near."

All this tale did Ulysses tell; but Eumæus doubted whether these things were so, thinking rather that the beggar-man said these things to please him. After this they talked much, and when the swineherd's men were returned they all feasted together. And the night being cold, and there being much rain, Ulysses was minded to see whether one would lend him a cloak; wherefore he told this tale—

"Once upon a time there was laid an ambush near to the city of Troy. And Menelaüs and Ulysses and I were the leaders of it. In the reeds we sat, and the night was cold, and the snow lay upon our shields. Now all the others had cloaks, but I had left mine behind at the ships. So when the night was three parts spent I spake to Ulysses, 'Here am I without a cloak; soon, methinks, shall I perish with the cold.' Soon did he bethink him of a remedy, for he was ever ready with counsel. Therefore to me he said, 'Hush, lest some one hear thee,' and to the others, 'I have been warned in a dream. We are very far from the ships, and in peril. Wherefore let some one run to the ships to King Agamemnon, that he send more men to help.' Then Thoas, son of Andræmon, rose up and ran, casting off his cloak, and this I took, and slept warmly therein. Were I this night such as then I was, I should not lack such kindness even now."

Then said Eumæus, "This is well spoken, old man. Thou shalt have a cloak to cover thee. But in the morning thou must put on thy own rags again. Yet perchance, when the son of Ulysses shall come, he will give thee new garments."

After this they slept, but Eumæus tarried without, keeping watch over the swine.

CHAPTER IX.

THE RETURN OF TELEMACHUS.

Now all this time Telemachus tarried in Sparta with King Menelaüs. To him went Athené, and warned him that he should return to his home, for that the suitors were devouring his substance, and that Penelopé, his mother, was much pressed by her father and her brothers to marry Eurymachus, who indeed of all the suitors promised the largest. Also she warned him that the suitors had laid an ambush to slay him in the strait between Samos and Ithaca, and that he should keep clear of the island; and as soon as ever he came near to Ithaca he should land and go to the swineherd Eumæus, and send him to his mother, with tidings of his being safely arrived.

Then Telemachus woke Pisistratus, and would have departed forthwith, only Pisistratus urged him that he should stay till the morning. So when the morning was come he would take leave of Menelaüs and Helen.

And first Menelaüs said that he would go with him through all the land of Greece, whithersoever he would; but seeing that his heart was steadfastly set to return to his home, he gave him gifts that he might take with him, and Helen also gave him a gift, the fairest robe that she had.

Then they departed; and that night they came to Pheræ, and lodged with Diocles, the son of Orsilochus, and the next night to Pylos, where old Nestor dwelt. And the next day, while they were doing sacrifice to Athené, behold! there came one Theoclymenus, a seer, who dwelt in Argos, and there had slain a man, wherefore he had fled; and now, seeing Telemachus, and hearing who he was, he prayed that he would receive him into his ship. Which thing Telemachus was willing to do. So the two departed together. And when they were come to Ithaca, Telemachus bade the men take the ship to the city, saying that he was minded to see his farms, but that in the evening he would come to the city, and would feast them with flesh and wine. And Theoclymenus he bade join himself to Eurymachus, who, he said, was the best of those that were suitors to his mother. And as he spake there appeared a hawk on his right hand, and it struck a dove, even between him and the ship.

Then the seer called him aside and said, "This is a sign from the gods. There is no house in Ithaca more to be feared than thine."

Then Telemachus was glad, and commended the seer to Piræus, who was the most faithful of his followers. After this the ship sailed to the city, but Telemachus went to the dwelling of the swineherd Eumæus. And Ulysses heard the steps of a man, and, as the dogs barked not, said to Eumæus, "Lo! there comes some comrade or friend, for the dogs bark not."

And as he spake, Telemachus stood in the doorway, and the swineherd let fall from his hand the bowl in which he was mixing wine, and ran to him and kissed his head and his eyes and his hands. As a father kisses his only son coming back to him from a far country after ten years, so did the swineherd kiss Telemachus. And when Telemachus came in, the false beggar, though indeed he was his father, rose, and would have given place to him; but Telemachus suffered him not. And when they had eaten and drunk, Telemachus asked of the swineherd who this stranger might be.

Then the swineherd told him as he had heard, and afterwards said, "I hand him to thee: he is thy suppliant; do as thou wilt."

But Telemachus answered, "Nay, Eumæus. For am I master in my house? Do not the suitors devour it? And does not my mother doubt whether she will abide with me, remembering the great Ulysses, who was her husband, or will follow some one of those who are suitors to her? I will give this stranger, indeed, food and clothing and a sword, and will send him whithersoever he will, but I would not that he should go among the suitors, so haughty are they and violent."

Then said Ulysses, "But why dost thou bear with these men? Do the people hate thee, that thou canst not avenge thyself on them? and hast thou not kinsmen to help thee? As for me, I would rather die than see such shameful things done in house of mine."

And Telemachus answered, "My people hate me not; but as for kinsmen, I have none, for Acrisius had but one son, Laertes, and he again but one, Ulysses, and Ulysses had none other but me. Therefore do these men spoil my substance without let, and, it may be, will take my life also. These things, however, the gods will order. But do thou, Eumæus, go to Penelopé, and tell her that I am returned, but let no man know thereof, for there are that counsel evil against me; but I will stay here meanwhile."

So Eumæus departed. But when he had gone Athené came, like a woman tall and fair; but Telemachus saw her not, for it is not given to all to see the immortal gods; but Ulysses saw her, and the dogs saw her, and whimpered for fear. She signed to Ulysses, and he went forth, and she said—

"Hide not the matter from thy son, but plan with him how ye may slay the suitors, and lo! I am with you."

Then she made his garments white and fair

and his body lusty and strong, and his face swarthy, and his cheeks full, and his beard black. And when he was returned to the house, Telemachus marvelled to see him, and said—

"Thou art not what thou wast. Surely thou art some god from heaven."

But Ulysses made reply, "No god am I, only thy father, whom thou hast so desired to see."

And when Telemachus yet doubted, Ulysses told him how that Athené had so changed him. Then Telemachus threw his arms about him, weeping, and both wept together for a while. And afterwards Telemachus asked him of his coming back. And Ulysses, when he had told him of this, asked him how many were the suitors, and whether they two could fight with them alone.

Then said Telemachus, "Thou art, I know, a great warrior, my father, and a wise, but this thing we cannot do; for these men are not ten, no, nor twice ten, but from Dulichium come fifty and two, and from Samos four and twenty, and from Zacynthus twenty, and from Ithaca twelve; and they have Medon the herald, and a minstrel also, and attendants."

Then said Ulysses, " Go thou home in the morning and mingle with the suitors, and I will come as an old beggar; and if they entreat me shamefully, endure to see it, yea, if they drag me to the door. Only, if thou wilt, speak to them prudent words; but they will not heed thee, for indeed their doom is near. Heed this also: when I give thee the token, take all the arms from the dwelling and hide them in thy chamber. And when they shall ask thee why thou doest thus, say that thou takest them out of the smoke, for that they are not such as Ulysses left behind him when he went to Troy, but that the smoke has soiled them. Say, also, that haply they might stir up strife sitting at their cups, and that it is not well that arms should be at hand, for that the very steel draws on a man to fight. But keep two swords and two spears and two shields—these shall be for thee and me. Only let no one know of my coming back—not Laertes, nor the swineherd, no, nor Penelopé herself."

But after a while the swineherd came back from the city, having carried his tidings to the queen. And this she also had heard from the sailors of the ships. Also the ship of the suitors which they had sent to lie in wait for the young man was returned. And the suitors were in great wrath and fear, because their purpose had failed, and also because Penelopé the queen knew what they had been minded to do, and hated them because of it.

CHAPTER X.

ULYSSES IN HIS HOME

THE next day Telemachus went to the city. But before he went he said to Eumæus that he should bring the beggar-man to the city, for that it was better to beg in the city than in the country. And the false beggar also said that he wished this. And Telemachus, when he was arrived, went to the palace and greeted the nurse Euryclea and his mother Penelopé, who was right glad to see him, but to whom he told nought of what had happened. And after this he went to Piræus, and bade him keep the gifts which King Menelaüs had given him till he should be in peace in his own house, and if things should fall out otherwise, that he should keep them for himself. And then he went to fetch the seer Theoclymenus, that he might bring him to the palace. And the seer, when he was come thither, prophesied good concerning Ulysses, how that he would certainly return and take vengeance for all the wrong that had been done to him.

Now in the meanwhile Eumæus and the false beggar were coming to the city. And when they were now near to it, by the fountain which Ithacus and his brethren had made, where was also an altar of the Nymphs, Melanthius the goatherd met them, and spake evil to Eumæus, rebuking him that he brought this beggar to the city. And he came near and smote Ulysses with his foot on the thigh, but moved him not from the path. And Ulysses thought a while, should he smite him with his club and slay him, or dash him on the ground. But it seemed to him better to endure.

But Eumæus lifted up his hands and said, "Oh, now may the Nymphs of the fountain fulfil this hope, that Ulysses may come back to his home, and tear from thee this finery of thine, wherein thou comest to the city, leaving thy flock for evil shepherds to devour!"

So they went on to the palace. And at the door of the court there lay the dog Argus, whom

ULYSSES & HIS DOG.

in the old days Ulysses had reared with his own hand. But ere the dog grew to his full, Ulysses had sailed to Troy. And, while he was strong, men used him in the chase, hunting wild goats and roe-deer and hares. But now he lay on a dunghill, and the lice swarmed upon him. Well he knew his master, and, for that he could not come near to him, wagged his tail and drooped his ears.

And Ulysses, when he saw him, wiped away a tear, and said, " Surely this is strange, Eumæus, that such a dog, being of so fine a breed, should lie here upon a dunghill."

And Eumæus made reply, " He belongeth to a master who died far away. For indeed, when Ulysses had him of old, he was the strongest and swiftest of dogs; but now my dear lord has perished far away, and the careless women tend him not. For when the master is away the slaves are careless of their duty. Surely a man, when he is made a slave, loses half the virtue of a man."

And as he spake the dog Argus died. Twenty years had he waited, and saw his master at the last.

After this the two entered the hall. And Telemachus, when he saw them, took from the basket bread and meat, as much as his hands could hold, and bade carry them to the beggar, and also to tell him that he might go round among the suitors, asking alms. So he went, stretching out his hand, as though he were wont to beg; and some gave, having compassion upon him and marvelling at him, and some asked who he was. But, of all, Antinoüs was the most shameless. For when Ulysses came to him and told him how he had had much riches and power in former days, and how he had gone to Egypt, and had been sold a slave into Cyprus, Antinoüs mocked him, saying—

"Get thee from my table, or thou shalt find a worse Egypt and a harder Cyprus than before."

Then Ulysses said, "Surely thy soul is evil though thy body is fair; for though thou sittest at another man's feast, yet wilt thou give me nothing."

But Antinoüs, in great wrath, took the stool on which he sat and cast it at him, smiting his right shoulder. But Ulysses stirred not, but stood as a rock. But in his heart he thought on revenge. So he went and sat down at the door. And being there, he said—

"Hear me, suitors of the queen! There is no wrath if a man be smitten fighting for that which is his own, but Antinoüs has smitten me because that I am poor. May the curse of the hungry light on him therefor, ere he come to his marriage day."

Also the other suitors blamed him that he had dealt so cruelly with this stranger. Also the queen was wroth when she heard it, as she sat in the upper chamber with her maidens about her.

But as the day passed on there came a beggar from the city, huge of bulk, mighty to eat and drink, but his strength was not according to his size. Arnæus was his name, but the young men called him Irus, because he was their messenger, after Iris, the messenger of Zeus. He spake to Ulysses—

"Give place, old man, lest I drag thee forth; the young men even now would have it so, but I think it shame to strike such an one as thee."

Then said Ulysses, "There is room for thee

and for me; get what thou canst, for I do not grudge thee aught, but beware lest thou anger me, lest I harm thee, old though I am."

But Irus would not hear words of peace, but still challenged him to fight.

And when Antinoüs saw this he was glad, and said, "This is the goodliest sport that I have seen in this house. These two beggars would fight; let us haste and match them."

And the saying pleased them; and Antinoüs spake again: "Hear me, ye suitors of the queen! We have put aside these paunches of the goats for our supper. Let us agree then that whosoever of these two shall prevail, shall have choice of these, that which pleaseth him best, and shall hereafter eat with us, and that no one else shall sit in his place."

Then said Ulysses, "It is hard for an old man to fight with a young. Yet will I do it. Only do ye swear to me that no one shall strike me a foul blow while I fight with this man."

Then Telemachus said that this should be so, and they all consented to his words. And after this Ulysses girded himself for the fight. And all that were there saw his thighs, how great

ULYSSES PREPARING TO FIGHT WITH IRUS.

and strong they were, and his shoulders, how broad, and his arms, how mighty. And they said one to another, "There will be little of Irus left, so stalwart seems this beggar-man." But as for Irus himself, he would have slunk out of sight, but they that were set to gird him compelled him to come forth.

Then said the Prince Antinoüs, "How is this, thou braggart, that thou fearest this old man, all woe-begone as he is? Hearken thou to this. If this man prevails against thee, thou shalt be cast into a ship and taken to the land of King Echetus, who will cut off thy ears and thy nose for his dogs to eat."

So the two came together. And Ulysses thought whether he should strike the fellow and slay him out of hand, or fell him to the ground. And this last seemed the better of the two. So when Irus had dealt his blow, he smote him on the jaw, and brake in the bone, so that he fell howling on the ground, and the blood poured amain from his mouth.

Then all the suitors laughed aloud. But Ulysses dragged him out of the hall, and propped him by the wall of the courtyard, putting a staff in his hand, and saying, "Sit there, and keep dogs and swine from the door, but dare not hereafter to lord it over men, lest some worse thing befall thee."

Then Antinoüs gave him a great paunch, and Amphinomus gave two loaves, and pledged him in a cup, saying, "Good luck to thee, father, hereafter, though now thou seemest to have evil fortune."

And Ulysses made reply, "O Amphinomus, thou hast much wisdom, methinks, and thy father, I know, is wise. Take heed, therefore. There is nought feebler upon earth than man. For in the days of his prosperity he thinketh nothing of trouble, but when the gods send evil to him, there is no help in him. I also trusted once in myself and my kinsmen, and now—behold me what I am! Let no man, therefore, do violence and wrong, for Zeus shall requite such deeds at the last. And now these suitors of the queen are working evil to him who is absent. Yet will he return some day and slay his enemies. Fly thou, therefore, while yet there is time, nor meet him when he comes."

So he spake, with kindly thought.

But his doom was on Amphinomus that he should die.

And that evening, the suitors having departed to their own dwellings, Ulysses and Telemachus took the arms from the hall, as they had also planned to do. And while they did so Telemachus said, "See, my father, this marvellous brightness that is on the pillars and the ceiling. Surely some god is with us."

And Ulysses made reply, "I know it: be silent. And now go to thy chamber and sleep, and leave me here, for I have somewhat to say to thy mother and her maidens."

And when the queen and her maidens came into the hall (for it was their work to cleanse it and make it ready for the morrow) Penelopé asked him of his family and his country. And at first he made as though he would not answer, fearing, he said, lest he should trouble her with the story of that which he had suffered. But afterwards, for she urged him, telling him what she herself had suffered, her husband being lost and her suitors troubling her without ceasing, he feigned a tale that should satisfy her. For he told her how that he was a man of Crete, a brother of King Idomeneus, and how he had given hospitality to Ulysses, what time he was sailing to Troy with the sons of Atreus.

And when the queen, seeking to know whether he spake the truth, asked him of Ulysses what manner of man he was, and with what clothing he was clothed, he answered her rightly, saying, "I remember me that he had a mantle, twofold, woollen, of sea-purple, clasped with a brooch of gold, whereon was a dog that held a fawn by the throat; marvellously wrought they were, so hard held the one, so strove the other to be free. Also he had a tunic, white and smooth, which the women much admired to see. But whether some one had given him these things I know not, for indeed many gave him gifts, and I also, even a sword and a tunic. Also he had a herald with him, one Eurybates, older than him, dark-skinned, round in the shoulders, with curly hair."

And Penelopé, knowing these things to be true, wept aloud, crying that she should see her husband no more. But the false beggar comforted her, saying that Ulysses was in the land of the Thresprotians, having much wealth with him, only that he had lost his ships and his comrades, yet nevertheless would speedily return.

Then Penelopé bade her servants make ready a bed for the stranger of soft mats and blankets, and also that one of them should bathe him. But the mats and blankets he would not have, saying that he would sleep as before; and for the bathing, he would only that some old woman, wise and prudent, should do this. Wherefore the queen bade Euryclea, the keeper of the house, do this thing for him, for that he had been the comrade of her lord, and indeed was marvellously like to him in feet and hands.

And this the old woman was right willing to do, for love for her master, " for never," she said, " of all strangers that had come to the land, had come one so like to him." But when she had prepared the bath for his feet, Ulysses sat by the fire, but as far in the shadow as he might, lest the old woman should see a great scar that was upon his leg, and know him thereby.

Now the scar had chanced in this wise. He had come to see his grandfather Autolycus, who was the most cunning of men, claiming certain gifts which he had promised to him in the old days when, being then newly born, he was set on his grandfather's knees in the halls of Laertes, and his grandfather had given him this name. And on the day of his coming there was a great feast, and on the day after a hunting on Mount Parnassus. In this hunting, therefore, Ulysses came in the heart of a wood upon a place where lay a great wild boar, and the beast, being stirred by the noise, rose up, and Ulysses charged him with his spear, but before he could slay the beast it ripped a great wound just above the knee. And afterwards Ulysses slew it, and the young men bound up the wound, singing a charm to stanch the blood.

By this scar, then, the old nurse knew that it was Ulysses himself, and said, "O Ulysses, O my child, to think that I knew thee not!"

And she looked towards the queen, as meaning to tell the thing to her. But Ulysses laid his hand on her throat, "Mother, wouldst thou kill me? I am returned after twenty years; and none must know till I shall be ready to take vengeance."

And the old woman held her peace. And after this Penelopé talked with him again, telling

EURYCLEA DISCOVERS ULYSSES.

him her dreams, how she had seen a flock of geese in her palace, and how that an eagle had slain them, and when she mourned for the geese, lo! a voice that said, "These geese are thy suitors, and the eagle thy husband."

And Ulysses said that the dream was well. And then she said that on the morrow she must make her choice, for that she had promised to bring forth the great bow that was Ulysses', and whosoever should draw it most easily, and shoot an arrow best at a mark, he should be her husband.

And Ulysses made answer to her, "It is well, lady. Put not off this trial of the bow, for before one of them shall draw the string the great Ulysses shall come and duly shoot at the mark that shall be set."

After this Penelopé slept, but Ulysses watched.

CHAPTER XI.

THE TRIAL OF THE BOW.

THE next day many things cheered Ulysses for that which he had to do; for first Athené had told him that she would stand at his side, and next he heard the thunder of Zeus in a clear sky, and last it chanced that a woman who sat at the mill grinding corn, being sore weary of her task, and hating the suitors, said, "Grant, Father Zeus, that this be the last meal which these men shall eat in the house of Ulysses!"

And after a while the suitors came and sat down, as was their wont, to the feast. And the servants bare to Ulysses, as Telemachus had bidden, a full share with the others. And when Ctesippus, a prince of Samos, saw this (he was a man heedless of right and of the gods), he said, "Is it well that this fellow should fare even as we? Look now at the gift that I shall give him." Whereupon he took a bullock's foot out of a basket wherein it lay, and cast it at Ulysses.

But he moved his head to the left and shunned it, and it flew on, marking the wall. And Telemachus cried in great wrath—

"It is well for thee, Ctesippus, that thou didst not strike this stranger. For surely, hadst thou done this thing, my spear had pierced thee through, and thy father had made good cheer, not for thy marriage, but for thy burial."

Then said Agelaüs, "This is well said. Telemachus should not be wronged, no, nor this stranger. But, on the other hand, he must bid his mother choose out of the suitors whom she will, and marry him, nor waste our time any more."

And Telemachus said, "It is well. She shall marry whom she will. But from my house I will never send her against her will."

And the suitors laughed; but their laughter was not of mirth, and the flesh which they ate dripped with blood, and their eyes were full of tears. And the eyes of the seer Theoclymenus were opened, and he cried—

"What ails you, miserable ones? For your

heads and your faces and your knees are covered with darkness, and the voice of groaning comes from you, and your cheeks are wet with tears. Also the walls and the pillars are sprinkled with blood, and the porch and the hall are full of shadows that move towards hell, and the sun has perished from the heaven, and an evil mist is over all."

But they laughed to hear him; and Eurymachus said, "This stranger is mad; let us send him out of doors into the market-place, for it seems that here it is dark."

Also they scoffed at Telemachus, but he heeded them not, but sat waiting till his father should give the sign.

After this Penelopé went to fetch the great bow of Ulysses, which Iphitus had given to him. From the peg on which it hung she took it with its sheath, and sitting down, she laid it on her knees and wept over it, and after this rose up and went to where the suitors sat feasting in the hall. The bow she brought, and also the quiver full of arrows, and standing by the pillar of the dome, spake thus—

"Ye suitors who devour this house, making

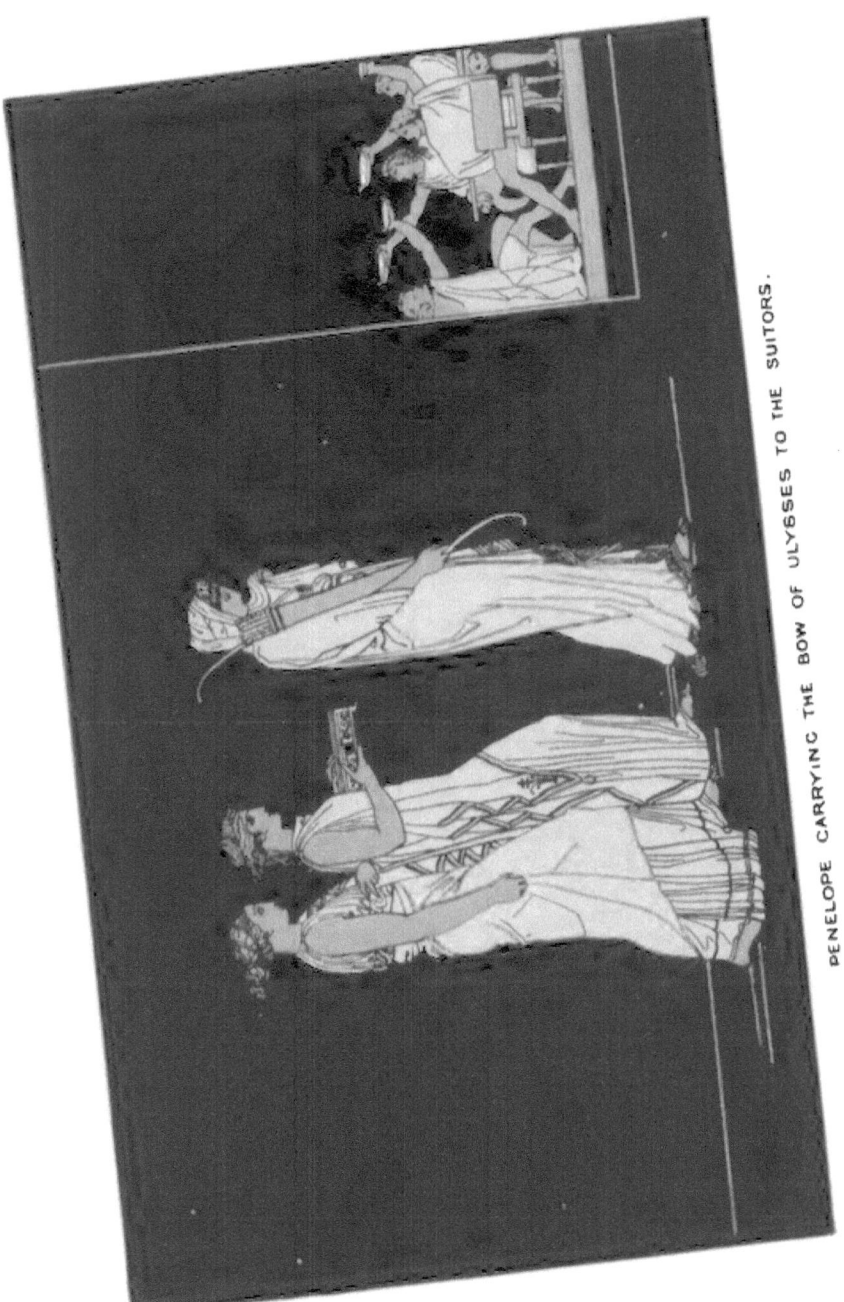

PENELOPE CARRYING THE BOW OF ULYSSES TO THE SUITORS.

pretence that ye wish to wed me, lo! here is a proof of your skill. Here is the bow of the great Ulysses. Whoso shall bend it easiest in his hands, and shoot an arrow most easily through the helve-holes of the twelve axes that Telemachus shall set up, him will I follow, leaving this house, which I shall remember only in my dreams."

Then she bade Eumæus bear the bow and the arrows to the suitors. And the good swineherd wept to see his master's bow, and Philœtius, the herdsman of the kine, wept also, for he was a good man, and loved the house of Ulysses.

Then Telemachus planted in due order the axes wherein were the helve-holes, and was minded himself to draw the bow; and indeed would have done the thing, but Ulysses signed to him that he should not. Wherefore he said, "Methinks I am too weak and young; ye that are elder should try the first."

Then first Leiodes, the priest, who alone among the suitors hated their evil ways, made trial of the bow. But he moved it not, but wearied his hands with it, for they were tender, and unwont to toil. And he said, "I cannot bend this bow; let some other try; but it shall be grief and pain to many this day, I trow."

And Antinoüs was wroth to hear such words, and bade Melanthius bring forth from the stores a roll of fat, that they might anoint the string and soften it withal. So they softened the string with fat, but not for that the more could they bend it, for they tried all of them in vain, till only Antinoüs and Eurymachus were left, who indeed were the bravest and the strongest of them all.

Now the swineherd and the herdsman of the kine had gone forth out of the yard, and Ulysses came behind them and said, "What would ye do if Ulysses were to come back to his home? Would ye fight for him, or for the suitors?"

And both said that they would fight for him.

And Ulysses said, "It is even I who am come back in the twentieth year, and ye, I know, are glad at heart that I am come; nor know I of any one besides. And if ye will help me as brave men to-day, wives shall ye have, and possessions and houses near to mine own. And ye shall be brothers and comrades to Telemachus. And for a sign, behold this scar, which the wild boar made when I hunted with Autolycus."

Then they wept for joy and kissed Ulysses, and he also kissed them. And he said to Eumæus that he should bring the bow to him when the suitors had tried their fortune therewith; also that he should bid the women keep within doors, nor stir out if they should hear the noise of battle. And Philætius he bade lock the doors of the hall, and fasten them with a rope.

After this he came back to the hall, and Eurymachus had the bow in his hands, and sought to warm it at the fire. Then he essayed to draw it, but could not. And he groaned aloud, saying, "Woe is me! not for loss of this marriage only, for there are other women to be wooed in Greece, but that we are so much weaker than the great Ulysses. This is indeed shame to tell."

Then said Antinoüs, "Not so; to-day is a holy day of the God of Archers; therefore we could not draw the bow. But to-morrow will we try once more, after due sacrifice to Apollo."

And this saying pleased them all; but Ulysses said, "Let me try this bow, for I would fain know whether I have such strength as I had in former days."

At this all the suitors were wroth, and chiefly Antinoüs, but Penelopé said that it should be so, and promised the man great gifts if he could draw this bow.

But Telemachus spake thus, "Mother, the bow is mine to give or to refuse. And no man shall say me nay, if I will that this stranger make trial of it. But do thou go to thy chamber with thy maidens, and let men take thought for these things."

And this he said, for that he would have her depart from the hall forthwith, knowing what should happen therein. But she marvelled to hear him speak with such authority, and answered not, but departed. And when Eumæus would have carried the bow to Ulysses, the suitors spake roughly to him, but Telemachus constrained him to go. Therefore he took the bow and gave it to his master. Then went he to Euryclea, and bade her shut the door of the women's chambers and keep them within, whatsoever they might hear. Also Philætius shut the doors of the hall, and fastened them with a rope.

Then Ulysses handled the great bow, trying it, whether it had taken any hurt, but the suitors thought scorn of him. Then, when he had found it to be without flaw, just as a minstrel fastens a string upon his harp and strains it to the pitch, so he strung the bow without toil; and holding the string in his right hand, he tried its tone, and the tone was sweet as the voice of a swallow. Then he took an arrow from the quiver, and laid the notch upon the string and drew it, sitting as he was, and the arrow passed through every ring, and stood in the wall beyond. Then he said to Telemachus—

"There is yet a feast to be held before the sun go down."

And he nodded the sign to Telemachus. And forthwith the young man stood by him, armed with spear and helmet and shield.

CHAPTER XII.

THE SLAYING OF THE SUITORS.

Then spake he among the suitors, "This labour has been accomplished. Let me try at yet another mark."

And he aimed his arrow at Antinoüs. But the man was just raising a cup to his lips, thinking not of death, for who had thought that any man, though mightiest of mortals, would venture on such a deed, being one among many? Right through the neck passed the arrow-head, and the blood gushed from his nostrils, and he dropped the cup and spurned the table from him.

And all the suitors, when they saw him fall, leapt from their seats; but when they looked, there was neither spear nor shield upon the wall. And they knew not whether it was by chance or of set purpose that the stranger had smitten him. But Ulysses then declared who he was, saying—

"Dogs, ye thought that I should never come back. Therefore have ye devoured my house, and made suit to my wife while I yet lived, and feared not the gods nor regarded men. Therefore a sudden destruction is come upon you all."

Then, when all the others trembled for fear, Eurymachus said, "If thou be indeed Ulysses of Ithaca, thou hast said well. Foul wrong has been done to thee in the house and in the field. But lo! he who was the mover of it all lies here, even Antinoüs. Nor was it so much this marriage that he sought, as to be king of this land, having destroyed thy house. But we will pay thee back for all that we have devoured, even twenty times as much."

But Ulysses said, "Speak not of paying back. My hands shall not cease from slaying till I have taken vengeance on you all."

Then said Eurymachus to his comrades, "This man will not stay his hands. He will smite us all with his arrows where he stands. But let us win the door, and raise a cry in the city; soon then will this archer have shot his last."

And he rushed on, with his two-edged knife in his hand. But as he rushed, Ulysses smote him on the breast with an arrow, and he fell forwards. And when Amphinomus came on, Telemachus slew him with his spear, but drew not the spear from the body, lest some one should smite him unawares.

Then he ran to his father and said, "Shall I fetch arms for us and our helpers?"

"Yea," said he, "and tarry not, lest my arrows be spent."

So he fetched from the armoury four shields and four helmets and eight spears. And he and the servants, Eumæus and Philætius, armed themselves. Also Ulysses, when his arrows were spent, donned helmet and shield, and took a mighty spear in each hand. But Melanthius, the goatherd, crept up to the armoury and brought down therefrom twelve helmets and shields, and spears as many. And when Ulysses saw that the suitors were arming themselves, he feared greatly, and said to his son—

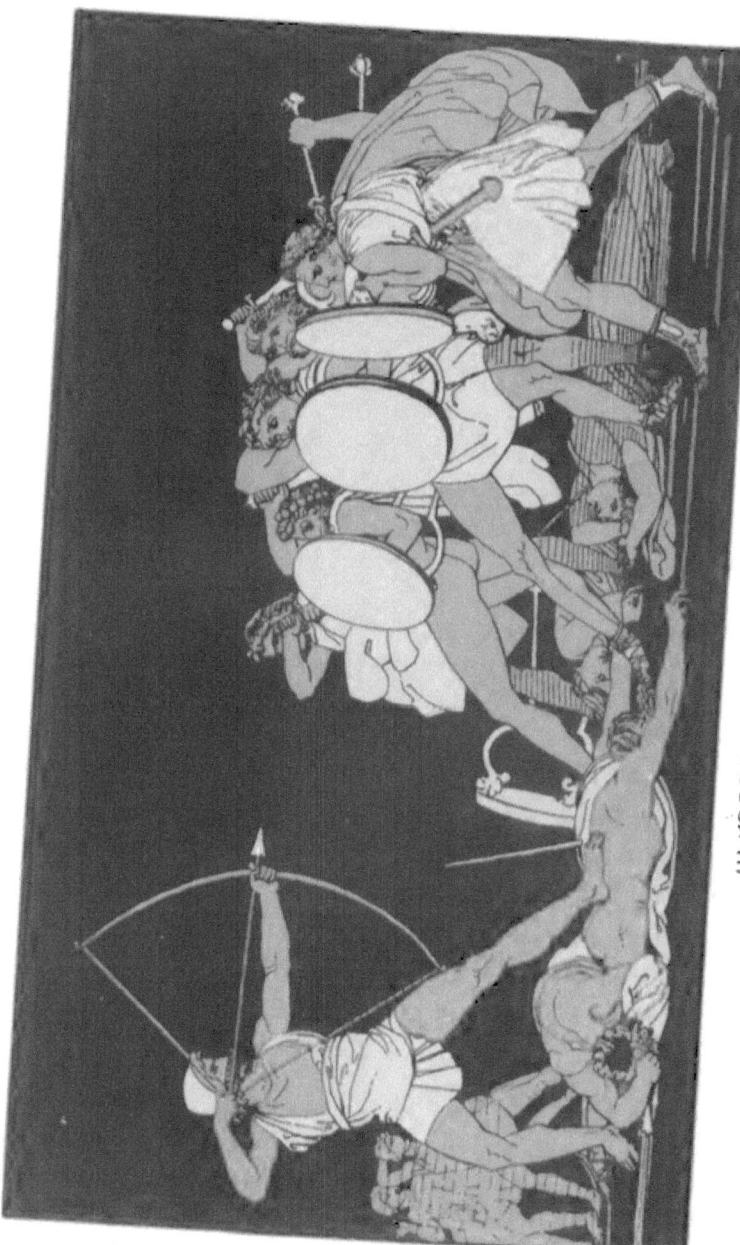

ULYSSES KILLING THE SUITORS.

"There is treachery here. It is one of the women, or, it may be, Melanthius, the goatherd."

And Telemachus said, "This fault is mine, my father, for I left the door of the chamber unfastened."

And soon Eumæus spied Melanthius stealing up to the chamber again, and followed him, and Philœtius with him. There they caught him, even as he took a helmet in one hand and a shield in the other, and bound his feet and hands, and fastened him aloft by a rope to the beams of the ceiling.

Then these two went back to the hall, and there also came Athené, having the shape of Mentor. Still, for she would yet further try the courage of Ulysses and his son, she helped them not as yet, but changing her shape, sat on the roof-beam like unto a swallow.

And then cried Agelaüs, "Friends, Mentor is gone, and helps them not. Let us not cast our spears at random, but let six come on together, if perchance we may prevail against them."

Then they cast their spears, but Athené

turned them aside, one to the pillar and another to the door and another to the wall. But Ulysses and Telemachus and the two herdsmen slew each his man; and yet again they did so, and again. Only Amphimedon wounded Telemachus, and Ctesippus grazed the shoulder of Eumæus. But Telemachus struck down Amphimedon, and the herdsman of the kine slew Ctesippus, saying, "Take this, for the ox foot which thou gavest to our guest." And all the while Athené waved her flaming ægis-shield from above, and the suitors fell as birds are scattered and torn by eagles.

Then Leiodes, the priest, made supplication to Ulysses, saying, "I never wrought evil in this house, and would have kept others from it, but they would not. Nought have I done save serve at the altar; wherefore slay me not."

And Ulysses made reply, "That thou hast served at the altar of these men is enough, and also that thou wouldest wed my wife."

So he slew him; but Phemius, the minstrel, he spared, for he had sung among the suitors in the hall, of compulsion, and not of good will; and also Medon, the herald, bidding them go into the yard without. There they sat, holding by the altar and looking fearfully every way, for yet they feared that they should die.

So the slaughtering of the suitors was ended; and now Ulysses bade cleanse the hall and wash the benches and the tables with water, and purify them with sulphur. And when this was done, that Euryclea, the nurse, should go to Penelopé and tell her that her husband was indeed returned. So Euryclea went to her chamber and found the queen newly woke from slumber, and told her that her husband was returned, and how that he had slain the suitors, and how that she had known him by the scar where the wild boar had wounded him.

And yet the queen doubted, and said, "Let me go down and see my son, and these men that are slain, and the man who slew them."

So she went, and sat in the twilight by the other wall, and Ulysses sat by a pillar, with eyes cast down, waiting till his wife should speak to him. But she was sore perplexed; for now she seemed to know him, and now she knew him not, being in such evil case, for he had not suffered that the women should put new robes upon him.

And Telemachus said, "Mother, evil mother, sittest thou apart from my father, and speakest not to him? Surely thy heart is harder than a stone."

But Ulysses said, "Let be, Telemachus. Thy mother will know that which is true in good time. But now let us hide this slaughter for a while, lest the friends of these men seek vengeance against us. Wherefore let there be music and dancing in the hall, so that men shall say, 'This is the wedding of the queen, and there is joy in the palace,' and know not of the truth."

So the minstrel played and the women danced. And meanwhile Ulysses went to the bath, and clothed himself in bright apparel, and came back to the hall, and Athené made him fair and young to see. Then he sat him down as before, over against his wife, and said—

"Surely, O lady, the gods have made thee harder of heart than all women besides. Would other wife have kept away from her husband, coming back now after twenty years?"

And when she doubted yet, he spake again, "Hear thou this, Penelopé, and know that it is

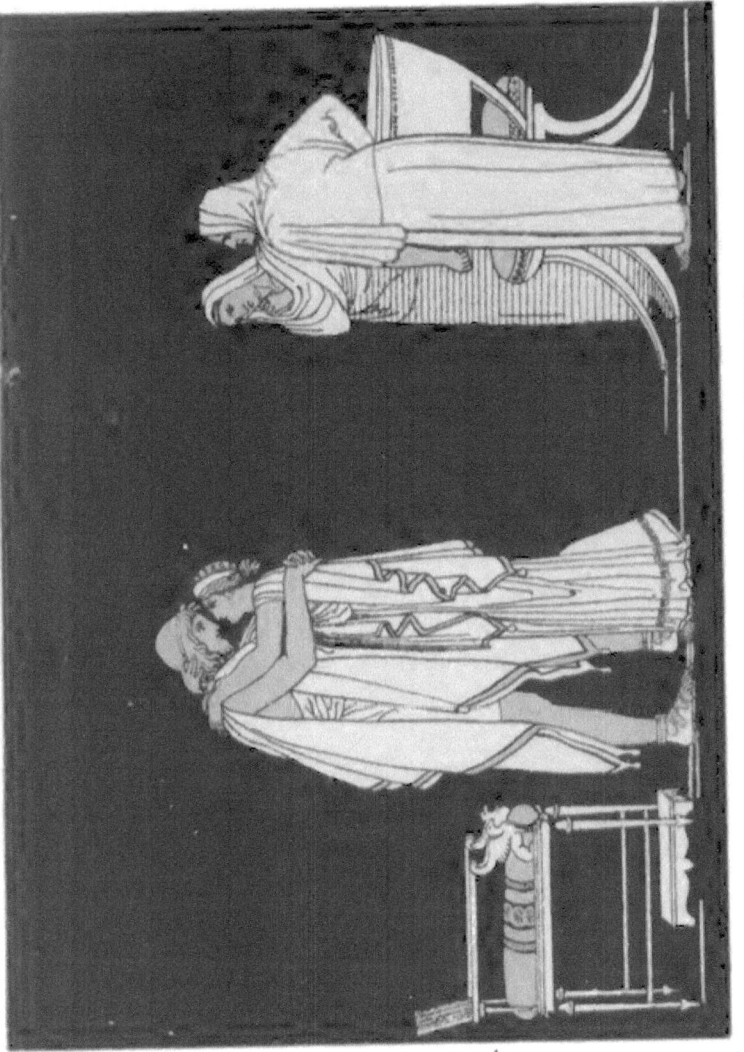

THE MEETING OF ULYSSES & PENELOPE

I myself, and not another. Dost thou remember how I built up the bed in our chamber? In the court there grew an olive tree, stout as a pillar, and round it I built a chamber of stone, and spanned the chamber with a roof; and I hung also a door, and then I cut off the leaves of the olive, and planed the trunk, to be smooth and round; and the bed I inlaid with ivory and silver and gold, and stretched upon it an oxhide that was ornamented with silver."

Then Penelopé knew him that he was her husband indeed, and ran to him, and threw her arms about him and kissed him, saying, "Pardon me, my lord, if I was slow to know thee; for ever I feared, so many wiles have men, that some one should deceive me, saying that he was my husband. But now I know this, that thou art he and not another."

And they wept over each other and kissed each other. So did Ulysses come back to his home after twenty years.

THE END.

BY THE SAME AUTHOR.

STORIES FROM VIRGIL.

WITH TWENTY ILLUSTRATIONS FROM DESIGNS BY PINELLI.

Crown 8vo., 3s. Cloth.

UNWIN BROTHERS, PRINTERS, CHILWORTH AND LONDON.

www.ingramcontent.com/pod-product-compliance
Lightning Source LLC
Chambersburg PA
CBHW021623250426
43672CB00037B/372